Student-Centered Coaching: The Moves

Student-Centered Coaching: The Moves

Diane Sweeney
Leanna S. Harris

FOR INFORMATION:

Corwin

A SAGE Company

2455 Teller Road

Thousand Oaks, California 91320

(800) 233-9936

www.corwin.com

SAGE Publications Ltd.

1 Oliver's Yard

55 City Road

London EC1Y 1SP

United Kingdom

SAGE Publications India Pvt. Ltd.

B 1/I 1 Mohan Cooperative Industrial Area

Mathura Road, New Delhi 110 044

India

SAGE Publications Asia-Pacific Pte. Ltd.

3 Church Street

#10-04 Samsung Hub

Singapore 049483

Program Director: Dan Alpert
Senior Associate Editor: Kimberly Greenberg
Editorial Assistant: Katie Crilley
Production Editor: Amy Schroller
Copy Editor: Michelle Ponce
Typesetter: C&M Digitals (P) Ltd.
Proofreader: Rae-Ann Goodwin
Indexer: Judy Hunt
Cover Designer: Anupama Krishnan
Marketing Manager: Charline Maher

Copyright © 2017 by Corwin

All rights reserved. When forms and sample documents are included, their use is authorized only by educators, local school sites, and/or noncommercial or nonprofit entities that have purchased the book. Except for that usage, no part of this book may be reproduced or utilized in any form or by any means, electronic or mechanical, including photocopying, recording, or by any information storage and retrieval system, without permission in writing from the publisher.

All trademarks depicted within this book, including trademarks appearing as part of a screenshot, figure, or other image, are included solely for the purpose of illustration and are the property of their respective holders. The use of the trademarks in no way indicates any relationship with, or endorsement by, the holders of said trademarks.

Cover image by Colin Brown. Used with permission.

Printed in the United States of America

ISBN 978-1-5063-2526-2

This book is printed on acid-free paper.

23 24 25 20 19 18 17

DISCLAIMER: This book may direct you to access third-party content via Web links, QR codes, or other scannable technologies, which are provided for your reference by the author(s). Corwin makes no guarantee that such third-party content will be available for your use and encourages you to review the terms and conditions of such third-party content. Corwin takes no responsibility and assumes no liability for your use of any third-party content, nor does Corwin approve, sponsor, endorse, verify, or certify such third-party content.

Contents

Acknowledgments	ix
About the Authors	xi
Introduction	**1**
Our Coaching Beliefs	1
Core Practices for Student-Centered Coaching	3
Student-Centered Coaching Is Driven by Formative Assessment Data	4
How Student-Centered Coaching Compares With Other Coaching Models	5
Moving Forward	7
Chapter 1: Setting Goals for Coaching Cycles	**9**
The Move—*Setting Goals for Coaching Cycles*	9
Why *Setting Goals for Coaching Cycles* Is Important	10
What *Setting Goals for Coaching Cycles* Looks Like	12
Lessons From the Field	20
Tools and Techniques	22
A Final Thought	23
Chapter 2: Using Learning Targets	**25**
The Move—*Using Learning Targets*	26
Why *Using Learning Targets* Is Important	26
What *Using Learning Targets* Looks Like	27
Lessons From the Field	33
Tools and Techniques	38
A Final Thought	41
Chapter 3: Getting Ready for Coaching in the Classroom	**43**
The Move—*Getting Ready for Coaching in the Classroom*	43
Why *Getting Ready for Coaching in the Classroom* Is Important	44
What *Getting Ready for Coaching in the Classroom* Looks Like	45

Lessons From the Field　　　　　　　　　　　52
　　　Tools and Techniques　　　　　　　　　　　55
　　　A Final Thought　　　　　　　　　　　　　56

Chapter 4: Noticing and Naming　　　　　　　59

　　　The Move—*Noticing and Naming*　　　　　　60
　　　Why *Noticing and Naming* Is Important　　　60
　　　What *Noticing and Naming* Looks Like　　　61
　　　Lessons From the Field　　　　　　　　　　　67
　　　Tools and Techniques　　　　　　　　　　　70
　　　A Final Thought　　　　　　　　　　　　　73

Chapter 5: Micro Modeling　　　　　　　　　75

　　　The Move—*Micro Modeling*　　　　　　　　76
　　　Why *Micro Modeling* Is Important　　　　　77
　　　What *Micro Modeling* Looks Like　　　　　78
　　　Lessons From the Field　　　　　　　　　　　82
　　　Tools and Techniques　　　　　　　　　　　85
　　　A Final Thought　　　　　　　　　　　　　88

Chapter 6: Thinking Aloud　　　　　　　　　89

　　　The Move—*Thinking Aloud*　　　　　　　　90
　　　Why *Thinking Aloud* Is Important　　　　　91
　　　What *Thinking Aloud* Looks Like　　　　　91
　　　Lessons From the Field　　　　　　　　　　　97
　　　Tools and Techniques　　　　　　　　　　　99
　　　A Final Thought　　　　　　　　　　　　　100

Chapter 7: Sorting Student Work　　　　　　103

　　　The Move—*Sorting Student Work*　　　　　104
　　　Why *Sorting Student Work* Is Important　　104
　　　What *Sorting Student Work* Looks Like　　105
　　　Lessons From the Field　　　　　　　　　　110
　　　Tools and Techniques　　　　　　　　　　　114
　　　A Final Thought　　　　　　　　　　　　　116

Chapter 8: Providing Strengths-Based Feedback　117

　　　The Move—*Providing Strengths-Based Feedback*　118
　　　Why *Providing Strengths-Based Feedback* Is Important　118
　　　What *Providing Strengths-Based Feedback* Looks Like　119
　　　Lessons From the Field　　　　　　　　　　123
　　　Tools and Techniques　　　　　　　　　　　128
　　　A Final Thought　　　　　　　　　　　　　131

Chapter 9: Measuring the Impact of Coaching   **133**
   The Move—*Measuring the Impact of Coaching*   134
   Why *Measuring the Impact of Coaching* Is Important   134
   What *Measuring the Impact of Coaching* Looks Like   136
   Lessons From the Field   142
   Tools and Techniques   144
   A Final Thought   148

In Closing   **149**

Appendix   **151**
   Resource A—If/Then Charts   151
   Resource B—Coaching Logs   156
   Resource C—Language Stems   158
   Resource D—Planning Tools   161
   Resource E—Agreements and Protocols   162
   Resource F—Results-Based Coaching Tool   165

References   **167**

Index   **169**

Acknowledgments

We first met each other in the fall of 1996 in the teacher's lounge at Harrington Elementary School in Denver. The rest, as they say, is history. Ours is a history full of friendship, adventure, and lots of learning. From amazing coaching experiences to those we would rather forget (but that taught us an awful lot). From having babies to raising teenagers. We have definitely been through a lot together over the past twenty years!

As educators, our shared history is built upon the wisdom of countless teachers, administrators, and coaches who we have worked with over the years. To each of them we are grateful for helping to shape us into the student-centered coaches that we are today.

Our more recent history is being made in schools and districts around the country and beyond. Many of those stories have been shared in this book. To every coach, principal, district administrator, and teacher with whom we work, we share our heartfelt appreciation for the opportunity to collaborate with you. Your successes, your trials and tribulations, and your thoughtful questions about this work have pushed our thinking and taught us more than you can possibly imagine.

Many of those questions led us to the idea of writing this book, which is truly built upon our own histories as coaches but also on the myriad of coaching conversations that we have been lucky enough to observe and that have been shared with us over the years. Collectively, all of these experiences have helped us coalesce our thinking into a series of coaching *moves* related to the core practices for student-centered coaching.

Specifically, this book would not have been possible without the help of a few key people: our team member Julie Wright for giving us such thoughtful, *strengths-based feedback*, our editor, Dan Alpert, for always having our backs and inspiring us to keep plugging away, and Dan Sweeney for keeping the rest of our work lives on track so we could focus on writing. Many thanks to each of you.

We are also incredibly thankful for everyone who helped make the video clips in this book a reality, and we are confident that they will provide a powerful tool to demonstrate the various coaching moves described in the book. Thank you to the incomparable Brooke O'Drobinak and the teachers at Arrupe Jesuit High School in Denver; to Sara Tierney, Amy Tharp, Allison Beindorff, Cindy Graybeal, and the teachers at Field, Franklin, and Peabody Elementary Schools in Littleton, Colorado; to Joy Casey, Krista Dean, Val McElhinney, Rich Patterson, Cindy Ritter, and the teachers at Stuart, Prairie View, and Vikan Middle Schools in Brighton, Colorado; to Matt McKinney and Julie Slattery for their guidance throughout the video process; and to the crew at Hidden Woods Media for making it a smooth and comfortable experience.

Our shared history started on that fateful day in the teachers' lounge and has led us to the writing of this book. Our sincere gratitude to each and every one of you who has been a part of the journey along with us.

PUBLISHER'S ACKNOWLEDGMENTS

Corwin gratefully acknowledges the contributions of the following reviewers:

Ann M. Lorey
Common Core Coach and
　Science Department Instructional Supervisor
Palo Alto School District
Palo Alto, CA

Ruthanne Munger
Instructional Coach
Test Intermediate School
Richmond, IN

Tanna Nicely
Principal
South Knoxville Elementary
Blaine, TN

About the Authors

Diane Sweeney is the author of the bestselling books, *Student-Centered Coaching: A Guide for K-8 Coaches and Principals* (2011) and *Student-Centered Coaching at the Secondary Level* (2013). Both books are grounded in the simple but powerful premise that coaching can be designed to more directly impact student learning. Her first book, *Learning Along the Way* (2003), shares the story of how an urban elementary school transformed itself to become a learning community.

Diane spends her time speaking and consulting for schools and educational organizations across the country. She is also an instructor for the University of Wisconsin, Madison. When she isn't working in schools, she loves to spend time outside with her family in Denver, Colorado.

Leanna S. Harris has worked as a teacher, coach, and consultant across grades K-12. She currently works with Diane Sweeney Consulting to help schools and districts implement student-centered coaching. Her work is based upon the belief that professional development for teachers is most effective when it is grounded in outcomes for student achievement—for every child, every day.

Leanna lives in Denver, Colorado, with her husband and three kids.

Introduction

With the publication of *Student-Centered Coaching* (2011) and *Student-Centered Coaching at the Secondary Level* (2013), Diane created a theoretical framework for supporting teachers by focusing on outcomes for students. This approach has taken off because it makes sense to increase student achievement and develop teacher capacity—all at the same time. Yet, as we work with schools and districts to implement student-centered coaching, we are continually asked, "But what does it really *look* like?" This book will answer that question by breaking down the practice of student-centered coaching into a collection of "coaching moves" that are used throughout the process.

OUR COACHING BELIEFS

While this book will drill down into the *moves* for student-centered coaching, we have also come to realize that they don't mean a lot if they aren't grounded in a set of beliefs about why we are here in the first place. Time and time again, we have circled back on our beliefs when we find ourselves struggling in our coaching.

The following question that was sent to Diane on Twitter underscores how our beliefs drive our work. You'll notice that Diane's response brought the coach right back to her beliefs and how they impact her work with teachers.

Message to Diane:

Can student-centered coaching work when a teacher does not have good classroom management nor her routines and procedures established? Should I work with the teacher first on classroom management/routines/procedures or dive in with student-centered coaching?

Diane's Response:

The key is that you work on a goal that the teacher has set. Not a goal that you think the teacher should set. In my experience, the teacher has to be an invested partner in the process. We find that while classroom management may be an entry point to coaching, we hope to see the standards driving our coaching cycles. That way we can make sure that we are impacting student learning.

Coach's Response:

Thank you! I have to change my mindset and be an advocate for change. We haven't necessarily been willing to give teachers, especially teachers who are struggling in certain areas, the opportunity to set their own goals. We tend to set the goals for the teachers and then work with the teachers to accomplish them. This, of course, is not always well received. Still trying to switch!

In reading this exchange, you may have picked up on the fact that the coach was feeling unsure about where to start with her coaching. Leading her back to the belief that teachers own their own work and set their own goals reminded her that we need to avoid the trap of "fixing" teachers—a belief that is essential when it comes to working honestly and authentically with adult learners.

We often ask teams of coaches to write down the beliefs that underpin their work with teachers. Sometimes we fear they may be wondering, "Why are we doing this? I thought I was going to learn strategies for coaching." Yet, we continue to find that reflecting on our beliefs is essential because they drive most every part of how we work with adult learners. Being clear about them, and then aligning them with our actions, is a powerful step toward being an effective coach. If you haven't written down your own beliefs, we suggest that you do so. Now we'd like to share ours.

1. Increased student achievement—for all students every day—is why we are here.

2. It's not our job to fix teachers or to be the expert on all things. Everyone brings varied experience and expertise to the table.

3. The goals of others drive our work. We can't tell people what to care about.

4. Our work is ongoing—it doesn't happen in single conversations.

5. Relationship is an important factor but not our goal.

6. We are smarter together, and collaboration is critical.

7. Everyone is a learner, and our work is never done.

8. We assume best intent. Everyone cares about kids and is doing the best job that they can.

CORE PRACTICES FOR STUDENT-CENTERED COACHING

There are seven core practices that are foundational to student-centered coaching. While these core practices have always been a part of our work, we now see them more clearly due to countless hours of implementing student-centered coaching in a variety of schools and districts. As you explore this book, you will notice that we touch on most of these core practices in a variety of ways, just like we would suggest you do in your own coaching work.

1. Organizing Coaching through Cycles

One-shot opportunities for professional development do little to improve student learning. Coaching cycles provide job-embedded professional development that is ongoing and data driven. Taking a more thorough approach to coaching provides both the time that students need to master the standard and the time that teachers need to develop their skill in delivering instruction that moves student learning forward. More on this in Chapters 1 and 3.

2. Setting Goals for Coaching Cycles

Coaching cycles are driven by goals for student learning rather than by what we think the teacher *should* be doing. This keeps coaching focused on student achievement and away from evaluation. More on this in Chapter 1.

3. Using Standards-Based Learning Targets

Learning targets create the criteria for measuring student growth. Using student-friendly learning targets ensures that we are focused and deliberate about what we teach and how we assess. More on this in Chapter 2.

4. Using Student Evidence to Co-Plan Instruction

Using student evidence means that we are formatively assessing on a continual basis. Looking at student evidence creates opportunities to make informed instructional decisions. We sort student work according to patterns and then deliver differentiated instruction that matches exactly where the students are on any given day. More on this in Chapters 4 and 7.

5. Co-Teaching with a Focus on Effective Instructional Practices

Student-centered coaching is based on a partnership approach where the teacher and coach work side-by-side with students. When coaches work in classrooms, it ought to be hard to tell the difference between the coach and teacher because they are equally as engaged in the instruction. More on this in Chapters 4, 5, and 6.

6. Measuring the Impact of Coaching on Student and Teacher Learning

We believe that coaches are obliged to make sure that their coaching is impacting student and teacher learning. We use the Results-Based Coaching Tool to support this process. More on this in Chapter 9.

7. Partnering with the School Leader

Coaches can't do this work without the support of the school leader. We often hear from coaches who are supported and making an enormous impact on student and teacher learning. Then we meet others who are feeling less than supported in their schools and having less successful results in their coaching. Developing this partnership is essential if we are to take full advantage of our role as coaches. If you are interested in this topic, we'd recommend you read *Student-Centered Coaching: A Guide for K-8 Coaches and Principals* (2011).

STUDENT-CENTERED COACHING IS DRIVEN BY FORMATIVE ASSESSMENT DATA

Carol Ann Tomlinson (2014) writes, "A great teacher is a habitual student of his or her students. A keen observer, the teacher is constantly watching what students do, looking for clues about their learning progress, and asking for input from students about their status" (p. 10).

The notion of formative assessment, and of the teaching and learning cycle in which we assess, plan, and teach, is fundamental to the implementation of student-centered coaching. We work with teachers to interpret their formative assessment data (or student evidence, as we prefer to call it) so that they can scaffold, support, and extend learning—in the next moment or in the next day's lesson.

While schools are awash in summative assessments and high stakes test results, we don't find these types of data to be particularly useful during coaching cycles. We understand that progress monitoring is an important piece of the bigger picture of school improvement; it just doesn't inform our coaching conversations.

With an emphasis on qualitative rather than quantitative, we can use data to guide us toward our next steps in the classroom. This continual use of student evidence is what allows us to ensure that students are progressing toward the standards.

HOW STUDENT-CENTERED COACHING COMPARES WITH OTHER COACHING MODELS

As you dig into this book, you may be wondering how student-centered coaching compares with other ways of delivering coaching. We define coaching as "student-centered," "teacher-centered," or "relationship-driven," and the figure below outlines each of these methods in terms of the role of the coach, the focus for coaching, the use of data and materials, how the coach is perceived, and the role of relationships. We find that starting here helps coaches and school leaders understand how student-centered coaching compares with other ways of approaching coaching.

More Impact on Students---Less Impact on Students

	Student-Centered Coaching	Teacher-Centered Coaching	Relationship-Driven Coaching
Role	The coach partners with teachers to design learning that is based on a specific objective for student learning.	The coach moves teachers toward implementing a program or set of instructional practices.	The coach provides support and resources to teachers.

(Continued)

(Continued)

	More Impact on Students ←――――――――――――→ **Less Impact on Students**		
	Student-Centered Coaching	**Teacher-Centered Coaching**	**Relationship-Driven Coaching**
Focus	The focus is on using data and student work to analyze progress and collaborate to make informed decisions about instruction that is differentiated and needs-based.	The focus is on what the teacher is, or is not, doing and addressing it through coaching.	The focus is on providing support to teachers in a way that doesn't challenge or threaten them.
Use of Data	Formative assessment data and student work are used to determine how to design the instruction. Summative assessment data is used to assess progress toward mastery.	Summative assessment data is used to hold teachers accountable, rather than as a tool for instructional decision making.	Data is rarely used in relationship-driven coaching.
Materials	Textbooks, technology, and curricular programs are viewed as tools for moving student learning to the next level.	The use of textbooks, technology, and curricular programs is the primary objective of the coaching.	Sharing access and information to textbooks, technology, and curricular programs is the primary focus of the coaching.
Perception of the Coach	The coach is viewed as a partner who is there to support teachers to move students toward mastery of the standards.	The coach is viewed as a person who is there to hold teachers accountable for a certain set of instructional practices.	The coach is viewed as a friendly source of support that provides resources when needed.
Role of Relationships	Trusting, respectful, and collegial relationships are a necessary component for all forms of coaching.		

© Sweeney (Corwin Press, 2013). All rights reserved.

While student-centered coaching focuses on student performance, teacher-centered coaching is framed by the theory that if we develop the technical expertise of teachers, then student achievement will increase as well. The focus is on guiding teachers to use a specific program or set of instructional practices. It often blurs the line between coaching and evaluating because the emphasis is on "getting people to do things" and may create distrust and resistance among teachers. Relationship-driven coaching is less about holding teachers accountable and more about providing them with resources and support. It often feels safer because the coach's role is about making the lives of teachers easier. And since coaches learn that resistance is often par for the course, some may choose to back off and provide a more resource-based style of coaching.

The approach that a school takes often depends on its philosophy about how to improve teaching and learning. It may also depend on the school culture and relationships that a coach has with teachers. It isn't uncommon for coaches to engage in all three types of coaching in a single school—or even on a single day. But one has to wonder: If we really want to ensure that our students are learning, doesn't it make sense to make coaching about them?

MOVING FORWARD

It is our hope that this book will provide a practical vision of what it looks like to engage in student-centered coaching across a rich array of contexts. We are often asked by coaches if they are "doing it right." This question can be a hard one to answer because every decision is based on so many factors that there really isn't a right or wrong way. Rather, it's about making decisions that stay true to your purpose and beliefs. We hope you will walk away from this book with a variety of coaching moves, along with an understanding of exactly what they look like and why they matter. But remember that your insights, experiences, and beliefs are just as important as anything that we share in these pages.

1 Setting Goals for Coaching Cycles

Goals provide us with much needed focus when we are faced with a sea of things that demand our attention. They also help us stay motivated to work hard. NFL coach Bill Parcells, who coached the New York Giants to two Super Bowl wins, once wrote, "When you set small, visible goals, and people achieve them, they start to get it into their heads that they can succeed" (Parcells, 2001). The same goes for student-centered coaching. Beginning our partnership with a goal helps us get clear on what we are about. It's how we help teachers (and students) get into their heads that they can succeed.

THE MOVE—*SETTING GOALS FOR COACHING CYCLES*

Our definition of coaching cycles has grown and changed over the decade in which we have been implementing student-centered coaching. If you have read *Student-Centered Coaching* (Sweeney, 2011) or *Student-Centered Coaching at the Secondary Level* (Sweeney, 2013), you probably understand the components of a coaching cycle. These have remained fairly consistent over the years. They include the following:

- A minimum of one weekly planning conversation to look at student work and design upcoming instruction
- One to three times per week for coaching in the classroom

What has evolved is our thinking around the length of a coaching cycle. Initially, we found ourselves in coaching cycles that lasted between six to nine weeks. A primary reason for this is we designed our cycles based on the school calendar. We divided the year into quarters and used these to set up our coaching cycles. This continues to be the approach taken in some of our schools. More recently, however, we see curriculum being organized into units of study that last approximately four to six weeks. We are finding that structuring our coaching around these units provides us with an approach to scheduling that is more aligned with the standards. While the length of coaching cycles may vary, the key is to organize coaching into a format that is ongoing and creates the conditions where coaches can identify their impact on teacher and student learning. Setting a goal for the coaching cycle helps the teacher and coach articulate what they hope the students will learn as a result of this partnership.

Teachers often assume that the entry point for coaching is identifying a goal for themselves, or that coaching is about all of the things that they *should* be doing in their classrooms. This typically surfaces at the beginning of a coaching cycle when teachers ask for support with a new initiative or instructional practice. It may sound like, "I should be asking more text-dependent questions, can you help me with that?," "I need to be doing a better job managing my students' behavior," or "I have to start using the new math program that our district purchased."

Rather than focusing on what a *teacher* should do, student-centered coaching is driven by a goal for *student* learning. In this way, we design coaching cycles that are based on moving student learning forward. Teacher learning, schoolwide goals, and district initiatives will always be a part of the coaching process and may even come in the form of a secondary goal that is more about instructional practice. But we have found that using the language "Students will . . ." ensures that we are student-centered in our goal-setting process. This alone is what starts us off on the right path.

Goal setting isn't always a straightforward process. It can be a tricky conversation where the teacher and coach move in and among ideas, wrestle with competing demands, and balance priorities before landing on something that is (1) standards based, (2) valued by the teacher, (3) the right size and scope, (4) measurable through formative assessment, and (5) robust enough to carry a teacher and coach across the stages in a coaching cycle (Figure 1.1).

WHY *SETTING GOALS FOR COACHING CYCLES* IS IMPORTANT

The moment we set a goal is the moment when we decide on the outcomes we are after. We seek standards-based goals because we have found that if

Figure 1.1 Stages in a Coaching Cycle

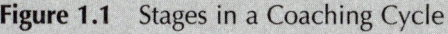

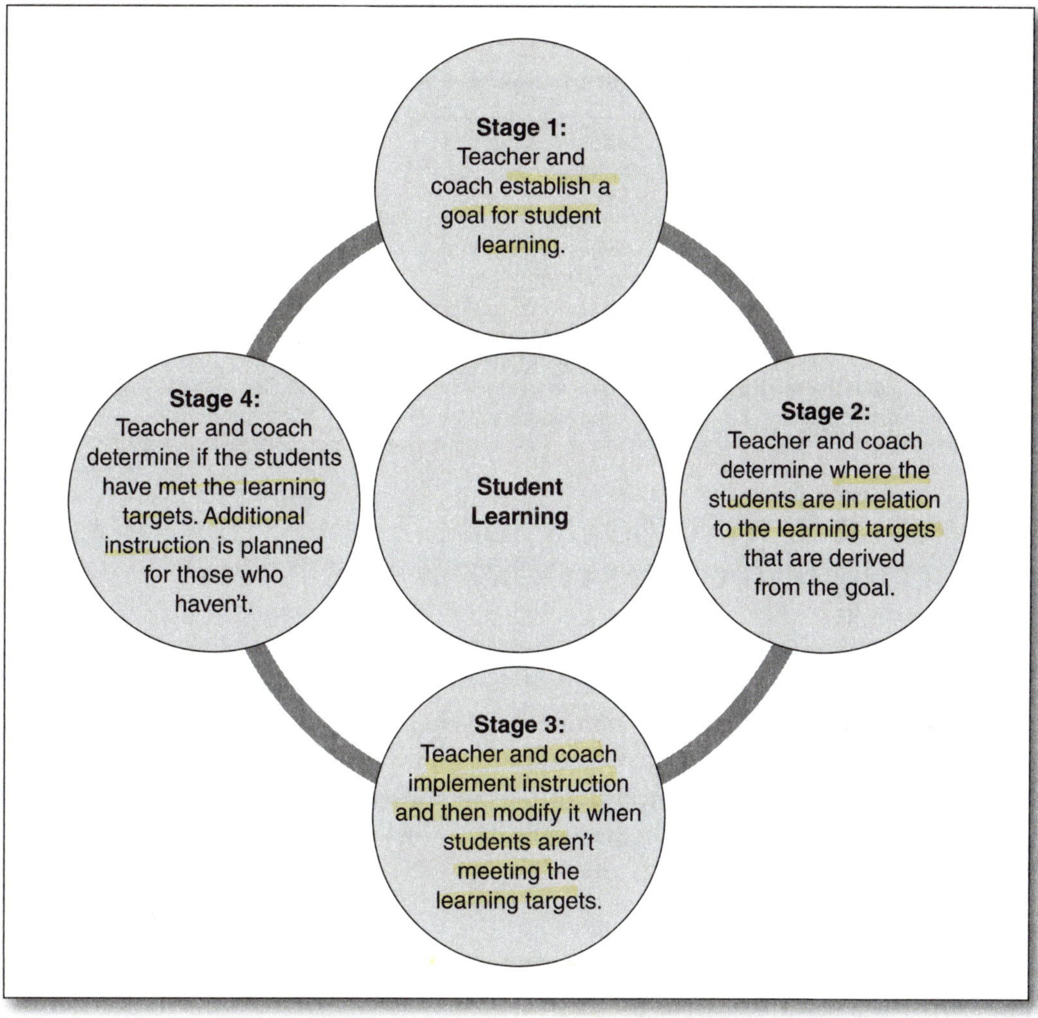

Stage 1: Teacher and coach establish a goal for student learning.

Stage 2: Teacher and coach determine where the students are in relation to the learning targets that are derived from the goal.

Stage 3: Teacher and coach implement instruction and then modify it when students aren't meeting the learning targets.

Stage 4: Teacher and coach determine if the students have met the learning targets. Additional instruction is planned for those who haven't.

Student Learning

coaching is relationship-driven, the goal tends to be about what the coach will do for the teacher. If coaching is teacher-centered, we are oriented around implementing a program or set of practices. If coaching is student-centered, we set a goal that points us toward the outcomes that we seek for students (Figure 1.2).

There are a lot of reasons to get smart about goal setting. A well-crafted goal goes a long way in surfacing what we value. When a goal is missing, we are unfocused and unable to recognize progress. With a goal, we are more prepared to identify growth among our students. We'd dare say that goal setting is so much a part of this work that without a goal we are no longer coaching.

Figure 1.2 How the Goal Defines a Coach's Role

More Impact on Students--Less Impact on Students

⬅➡

	Student-Centered Coaching	Teacher-Centered Coaching	Relationship-Driven Coaching
Role	The coach partners with teachers to design learning that is based on a specific set of learning targets.	The coach moves teachers toward implementing a program or set of instructional practices.	The coach provides support and resources to teachers.
Goal	The goal for coaching begins with the language, "The students will . . . "	The goal for coaching begins with the language, "The teacher will . . . "	The goal for coaching begins with the language, "The coach will . . . "

WHAT *SETTING GOALS FOR COACHING CYCLES* LOOKS LIKE

Leading effective goal-setting conversations takes practice. We prepare by developing an understanding of the standards and curriculum so that we can support teachers to name a goal that they care about. We use strategies such as listening, probing, and paraphrasing so that we hear, and then build on, the concerns of teachers. The following recommendations are drawn from goal-setting conversations that we've engaged in across grades K–12.

Set Goals With Teachers, Not for Them

Since coaching is about establishing partnerships with teachers, then goal setting is the perfect time to send a message that you are there to help teachers reach *their* goals for students. In the book *Instructional Coaching*, Jim Knight (2007) writes, "Partnership at its core, is a deep belief that we are no more important than those with whom we work, and that we should do everything we can to respect that equality. This approach is built around the core principles of equality, choice, voice, dialogue, reflection, praxis, and reciprocity" (p. 24). When we help teachers set goals that they feel are important, we honor the principles of true partnership.

It's never a good idea to set goals for teachers, even if we think we know what's best for them. Goals are personal, and the ownership rests with whoever will be doing the work to get there. While this may seem obvious, we are often tempted to nudge teachers toward a goal that we think is important, especially when we see the teaching and learning close up. After spending time in a teacher's classroom, we may be thinking, "I know the teacher wants to work on (fill in the blank). But we can't do that until we get (fill in the blank) under control." The temptation to redirect a teacher toward a goal that he or she hasn't named may come from a sincere concern for students. But going there may jeopardize the coaching cycle that we are trying to get started and the partnership that will help it succeed.

Use the Language "Students will . . . " to Help Teachers Frame Goals for Coaching

Goal-setting conversations aren't necessarily straightforward or predictable. Sometimes the coach is handed a goal on a silver platter, and other times it feels like a conversation loaded with land mines. In the following example, the teacher is clearly frustrated with her students' abilities. But rather than falling into that trap, the coach works hard to reframe the coaching partnership in a way that honors the concerns of the teacher but doesn't stay there (Figure 1.3).

Figure 1.3 Middle School Goal-Setting Conversation

Coach:	I'm looking forward to working with you during our upcoming coaching cycle. What goal for student learning would you like to focus on?
Teacher:	Well, it's my kids. They are so low. They can't read the novel I'm planning to teach. Other than reading it to them, I'm not sure what to do.
Coach:	Okay, so it sounds like you'd like to focus on reading. (*Pulls out the reading standards*)
Teacher:	I guess . . . but it's really just the novel.
Coach:	Got it. How about if we look at the standards for eighth grade and see where they fit with the literature you've selected. If we know what you'd like the students to do as readers, then we will be able to figure out what our work will look like.
Teacher:	We are reading historical fiction in the next unit. So we could look at that standard.
Coach:	(*Refers to standards*) They need to understand the structure of the plot, how the characters influenced the story, and different points of view. Which of these parts of the standard stand out to you?
Teacher:	Well, I like the idea of thinking about the characters.

(Continued)

Figure 1.3 (Continued)

Coach:	Ok . . . so how about going after a goal focusing on how the characters' qualities influenced the theme of the book? And we could even include different points of view.
Teacher:	I guess, as long as you can also help me with what to do about the lower readers.
Coach:	Definitely, we will work on how to scaffold and differentiate. We can even try using small groups and include some other short texts. There are a lot of instructional practices that we can use to support your struggling readers. Sound okay?
Teacher:	(*Sighs*) Okay. But that sounds like a lot.
Coach:	For now, we just have to envision our goal. We'll do the rest one day at a time. Can I just make sure I got this down correctly? Our goal is "Students will understand how fictional characters influence the theme of the book." What do you think?
Teacher:	That will work. Hopefully we can meet again to plan for my lower readers.
Coach:	Absolutely. How about if we meet on Friday to create a short reading assessment that will surface some of their needs? Then we can plan what to do next.

As you read the goal-setting conversation, you may have noticed some of the challenges that the coach was facing. While the teacher brought up concerns that were probably quite valid, they didn't necessarily translate into a motivating goal for a coaching cycle. Rather than letting the teacher's concern for her "lower readers" take over the conversation, the coach reframed it as being about differentiating and scaffolding. She even dropped in a few examples of what this might look like in practice. This way the coach honored the teacher's concerns and created a vision for how they would get past it.

Sometimes we find ourselves in a goal-setting conversation that focuses entirely on a new program or curriculum (Figure 1.4). As you read the next example, notice how the coach nudges the teacher away from perceiving her as a resource provider and toward the idea of a partner who is focused on standards-based instruction.

In this example, the coach was careful to nudge the conversation away from the activities in the math program and toward the student learning that they were after. Referring to the unit was a great start, but the coach also named their purpose as being about "teaching and assessing." She asked the teacher what she wanted the students to learn as a result of the unit, so they quickly moved beyond activities and toward learning.

Figure 1.4 Elementary School Goal-Setting Conversation

Coach:	I'm looking forward to working with you during our upcoming coaching cycle. You probably remember that we always start by determining a student-learning goal for our coaching cycle. What are you thinking?
Teacher:	I'm not sure about a student-learning goal. What I really need help with is a math unit coming up in two weeks that I've never taught. I need help with resources, strategies, and some formative assessment ideas. If you can get me those, then I should be ready to go.
Coach:	It's great that you are thinking through the unit ahead of time. Let's take a minute to review the unit so that we are clear about the learning we are after for your students. *(Coach pulls out the unit and standards)*
Teacher:	Ok, but what I really need is resources and activities.
Coach:	We'll definitely brainstorm resources and activities, but we need to start with a goal for student learning. That's key to understanding how we will teach and assess. It will also help us stay focused on your students.
Teacher:	Well, I suppose the goal is for my students to correctly add and subtract three digit numbers. I'd like them to do this quickly and from memory.
Coach:	Okay, that makes sense. As I look at the unit, I notice an emphasis on using a variety of strategies for solving these types of problems. For example, using place value, breaking apart numbers, and so on. What if we focused on helping your students use more strategies than just memorization? If we went in this direction, then we'd be right in line with the unit.
Teacher:	I guess more strategies would be okay. I just want them to get the correct answer and not count on their fingers anymore.
Coach:	I agree that the correct answer is important. How about if we make our goal for student learning something like "Students will understand and use a variety of strategies to correctly add and subtract three digit numbers." Would that goal work for you?
Teacher:	Sure, as long as I get some ideas for activities, too. That's really where I'm stuck.
Coach:	Of course! You'll remember that we have a weekly planning session as part of our coaching cycle. We'll do lots of planning together. We can also co-teach some lessons to try out some different ways to teach the lessons. Sound ok?
Teacher:	Sounds great. I'm excited to get started.

The coach was also careful to let the teacher know that she was hearing her concerns and reminded her that they will have lots of opportunities to co-plan and co-teach lessons. In this way, the coach honored the teacher and also made the coaching about student outcomes.

Use the Standards During Goal-Setting Conversations

The standards anchor most of our coaching cycles. This is how we ensure that the bulk of our coaching is focused on the knowledge and skills that are demanded of our students. Without the standards, we run the risk of identifying a goal that is too broad, too narrow, or not grade-level appropriate. With the standards, we are able to name a goal that is clearly aligned with what we want the students to know and be able to do.

We are often asked how to handle situations when teachers would like to focus on student engagement or behavior rather than any given standard. While we understand the importance of designing instruction that engages students, we don't see this as something that is separate from academics. For this reason, we like to steer teachers toward standards-based goals. We worry that if we isolate and coach into behavior, then we may end up looking at things like time-on-task rather than the learning that occurred. We'd rather put our effort toward engaging students through high quality and compelling work. As Phillip Schlechty (2011) suggests, a primary component of engagement is this: "The engaged student finds meaning and value in the tasks that make up the work" (p. 14).

As you might expect, there are exceptions to this rule. We understand that the teacher has to care about, and take ownership, over the goal. This means that there are times when we find ourselves in coaching cycles that focus less on the standards and more on engagement or behavior. For example, Diane recently worked with a group of special education coaches in the Denver area. They were working with teachers on managing behavior, helping students use assistive technology, and working with students to stay engaged throughout the day. Given their student population, the teachers were squarely focused on behavior and engagement. Rather than forcing the issue, and since goal setting demands that we be responsive to teachers, it didn't make sense to only focus on the standards. Instead, this team found more success setting goals for students around engagement and behavior. Would we like to see a focus on standards? Of course we would. And sometimes there is a follow-up opportunity to work on a standards-based goal after a cycle like this. But either way we understand that coaching is a partnership, and one of our primary beliefs is that the teacher has to be the one to set the goal for the coaching cycle. For more on the differences between standards-based goals and goals focusing on behavior or engagement, refer to *Student-Centered Coaching at the Secondary Level* (Sweeney, 2013).

Set Goldilocks Goals

If a goal is going to make the desired impact, then it ought to be just the right size and scope. We like to think of this as setting "Goldilocks goals," or goals that are just right. Figure 1.5 provides examples of goals that are too narrow, too broad, and just right.

Figure 1.5 Examples of Goldilocks Goals

Too Narrow	Just Right	Too Broad
Students will create a diagram that shows the water cycle.	Students will synthesize research in order to understand how drought impacts daily life.	Students will understand how weather works.
Students will learn their addition and subtraction facts.	Students will use a variety of strategies to solve two-digit addition and subtraction problems.	Students will understand the concept of addition and subtraction.
Students will memorize the major events in the Civil Rights movement.	Students will analyze the role of a key person in the Civil Rights movement.	Students will learn about the Civil Rights movement.

You may have noticed that our examples of "just-right goals" revolve around processes that involve reading, writing, or solving problems. This allows us to work with teachers to apply content knowledge in authentic ways. We understand the importance of learning content; we just don't view content knowledge as an ideal goal for a coaching cycle. For example, "learning your addition and subtraction facts" targets content. So does, "memorizing the major events in the Civil Rights movement." If these were goals for coaching cycles, then we would be limiting the outcome to learning discrete facts. Instead, we prefer goals that include content but also get at a deeper level of understanding.

When goals are too broad, such as "Students will learn about the Civil Rights movement," then we run the risk of kicking off a coaching cycle with little focus. We know that the scope is just about right when a goal leads us to generate between five and seven learning targets that capture the knowledge and skills we are after. It would be hard to accomplish this with a goal as broad as learning about the Civil Rights movement. But it would be possible if our goal was "Students will analyze the role of a key person in the Civil Rights movement," or "Students will read a collection of texts on the Civil Rights movement in order to create an argument for either side of the conflict." Having a clear sense of what the students should know and be able to do is essential for a goal to feel motivating and manageable. It is also essential for a coaching cycle to make the desired impact.

QR Code 1.1

Setting a Goal With a High School English Teacher

http://qrs.ly/bz5cdtc

QR Code 1.2

Setting a Goal for Secondary Coaching Cycles

http://qrs.ly/zy59nu7

Focus on the Learning Instead of the Task

We also avoid setting goals that are task or project oriented, such as "Students will create a diagram that shows the water cycle." Task-oriented goals are limiting because they are measured by whether the students *did* something instead of if they *learned* something.

This is a common experience faced by technology coaches. For example, a teacher is about to begin her tried-and-true unit on rocks and minerals that culminates with a museum where the students share their own rock collections. It is quite possible that when asked, the teacher will name a goal for coaching that sounds something like "I would like help with the student-led museum that we will be doing at the end of the unit. You know a lot about technology, maybe our goal can be to have the students create their projects using technology instead of the old-fashioned posters that we've done in the past." Right about now is when the coach recognizes that a shift of focus is required. The trick is doing so in a way that respects the teacher's request to "create a product" but also moves coaching to a more rigorous and student-centered place. Asking the teacher "What would you like the students to know and be able to do?" is a great way to move the focus away from creating a product. And if that doesn't work, it's time to pull out the standards so that the teacher is thinking about the knowledge and skills that she is after.

The Goal Is a Starting Point . . . Not the End Game

We are often asked how our goal-setting process compares with developing SMART goals. While we see the value of SMART goals in the context of school improvement plans and other big picture measures for accountability, we take a narrower approach that is often related to a unit of study or specific content area rather than on a certain amount of improvement on a specific assessment. Goals for coaching cycles are about what we'd like our students to learn over the next four to six weeks, rather than how we are going to show progress across the whole year.

Goals for coaching cycles are a lot like when the horses line up at the Kentucky Derby. They are in the starting gates, they are excited, and they know the direction they are headed. That's enough for now because our next step will be to unpack the goal into learning targets so that we will be able to evaluate how students are performing throughout the coaching cycle. This will be the focus of Chapter 2.

Keep the Focus on Students . . . and on Instruction

As we mentioned earlier, for goal setting to be effective, it begins with the standards. While we steer coaching toward standards-based goals, we also understand that an outcome for coaching is to help teachers refine their instructional practice. After all, we wouldn't be doing our job if we didn't help teachers get better at the instruction that they deliver on a daily basis. Instruction is how we move student learning forward.

We find that our goal-setting process sometimes includes a conversation about how we will use certain instructional practices to reach the goal that we set. This may be inspired by a pending (or past) evaluation. Or it may align with the instructional practices that are expected throughout the district. We often suggest districts get clear about their instructional expectations so that coaching can be more about support than about telling teachers what they *should* be doing. For example, we are currently working with a district that is targeting the following instructional practices: (1) decreasing lecture and increasing student discussion, (2) differentiating instruction using small groups, and (3) providing feedback to students. The coaches have found that they can easily embed the expected instructional practices right into their coaching cycles and remain focused on the standards. While these things aren't the goal for the coaching cycle, they are helpful to refer to during the goal-setting process.

Manage Goal Setting With Groups of Teachers

QR Code 1.3
Setting a Goal for a Coaching Cycle With a First-Grade Team

http://qrs.ly/u159nu9

Student-centered coaching isn't just about working with individual teachers. In fact, there are many advantages to working with groups of teachers during coaching cycles. Coaching groups of teachers increases the level of collaboration and is an efficient way to extend the coach's reach. We have found that small group coaching cycles are ideally made up of two to four teachers. Sometimes they are informal groupings, and other times they may be comprised of grade-level teams or departments. In either case, small group coaching cycles also begin with a goal for student learning.

At times, setting goals with groups of teachers is a piece of cake. The teachers are on the same page. They are predisposed to working together. And they are focused on moving student learning forward. In these cases, the coach may simply need to take the pulse of each group member to confirm that the goal feels right. This may sound like "Let's make sure this goal feels right before we commit to moving forward together."

At other times, setting goals with groups of teachers can be extremely challenging. This often occurs when groups of teachers aren't on the same page, are confrontational, or have different philosophies about teaching and learning. We find that in these situations, it's best for the coach to engage the group in an open-ended conversation that surfaces what they would like their students to know and be able to do and to refer to the standards to anchor the conversation. If we hope to create a sense of shared ownership and agreement about the goal, it is important for each individual to verbally state his or her commitment or name any concerns he or she might have. We suggest moving around the table to hear from every group member and using the questions "How do you feel about the goal that is on the table? Can you get behind it or do you have reservations?" If there is disagreement about the goal, the coach may choose to continue the goal-setting process or decide not to pursue the small-group coaching cycle at that time. We make this decision based on whether the group is able to name a student-centered goal that everyone can support. If not, it's probably a good idea to rethink the coaching cycle and provide other options for support such as individual coaching cycles, a group coaching cycle at a later date, a coaching cycle with a different combination of people, or support through professional learning communities (PLCs) or data teams. There is nothing wrong with adjusting the plan, especially if it is off track right from the beginning.

LESSONS FROM THE FIELD

Margaret is new to her district. After attending a recent session on student-centered coaching, she reached out to Diane for help. She was having a hard time getting her footing during a coaching cycle with a second-grade teacher. She had set up a coaching cycle, worked with the teacher to establish a goal, used effective questioning, and co-taught with the teacher in her classroom. But still, she was finding that the teacher was becoming less engaged as the cycle progressed. At first the teacher claimed that she "wanted direct feedback from Margaret." But later, she stated that she "had already done" what Margaret was suggesting. An unspoken tension had developed between Margaret and the teacher, and she wrote to Diane for help.

Diane's first question was "What was the goal that the teacher named for the coaching cycle?" It's no surprise that Diane started here because we have learned that when most coaching cycles go off track, it almost always comes down to the goal. Is the goal (1) standards-based, (2) valued by the teacher, (3) the right size and scope, (4) measurable through formative assessment, and (5) robust enough to carry a teacher and coach across the stages in a coaching cycle?

Margaret explained that at the beginning of the coaching cycle, the teacher had said she wanted to work on retelling and the Gradual Release of Responsibility, particularly helping students engage independently in their reading work. Diane thought that this seemed like the perfect opportunity to focus on retelling as their main goal and the gradual release as their secondary focus on instructional practice. It seemed like they were off to a good start. So what went wrong? Diane had to dig a little deeper.

As she continued to read Margaret's e-mail, the following line jumped out at her: "When I began to observe in her room, I noticed that behavior was a huge barrier to her making it to the independent practice part of each lesson. I was thinking that I would suggest embedding some work on behavior before we tackled retelling." Diane immediately recognized a common misstep. The original goal wasn't based on student behavior. But as Margaret spent time in the classroom, she began to view behavior as a problem, a problem that she worried would need to be solved before they could move forward with the goal that had been set. She tried to carefully raise the issue with the teacher in an attempt to help her reflect on how they might tackle this problem, but when she did this, she set aside the teacher's goal and introduced her own. While Margaret was probably 100% accurate in her belief that behavior wasn't where it should be, she had stepped into risky territory. Once a goal is set, it is incumbent upon us to maintain focus on the goal. If we stray, then we introduce our own agenda, and in turn, may alienate the teacher. Our ethic as coaches is that we are here to help teachers reach *their goals* for students. To do so, we have to stay focused on what they bring to the table.

Diane wrote back to Margaret and suggested that she bring the focus back to retelling. After all, this is what the students need to know and be able to do. She thought that if Margaret unpacked the standard by creating a set of learning targets with the teacher, then they would be in a better position to work side by side to implement instruction that increases student ownership and reduces behavior problems.

Margaret took this suggestion to heart and went back to the teacher, prepared with the plan of centering their work back on the standard of retelling. The teacher recommitted, and they saw the coaching cycle through. In the end, they were able to celebrate student growth and solidify instruction that is based on the gradual release of responsibility. Behavior improved and so did the students' ability to retell texts.

TOOLS AND TECHNIQUES

Troubleshooting Goals

The following if/then chart provides common scenarios that coaches face when engaging in goal-setting conversations (Figure 1.6).

Figure 1.6 Language for Goal-Setting Conversations

If I hear . . .	Then I can use the following language . . .
My students can't do anything.	What is your next unit of study? Let's take a look at the standards, and then we can figure out how to scaffold for them as learners.
I'm supposed to be using effective questioning techniques. It's on my evaluation.	That's great. We can tackle that during our coaching cycle. But let's first set a goal for your students.
I really just want you to lend me a hand. My class is out of control.	I will definitely lend you a hand when I'm in your room, but our work should focus on a goal for students. What's coming up next in your curriculum?

Coaching Log: Identifying a Goal for Student Learning

We have found that it's always a good idea to go into a goal-setting conversation with a plan. We suggest that coaches create a shared document, or coaching log, that begins with the goal-setting conversation. Our coaching log includes the following questions to scaffold the goal-setting process (Figure 1.7).

Figure 1.7 Coaching Log: Identifying a Goal for Student Learning

1. What goal for student learning will we go after during the coaching cycle?
2. How does the goal connect with the standards?
3. How does the goal connect with our curriculum and materials?

Open-Ended Questions for Goal Setting

There is a conversational flow and tone to setting goals with teachers. We use open-ended questions to encourage teachers to own the goals that they set. We also do a lot of listening so that we honor teachers by asking them to green light whatever goal is selected. The following questions provide teachers with ownership over the goals that they set.

1. What do you hope the students will learn as a result of our partnership?
2. Let's look at the standards. How might they help us choose a focus?
3. What would you like to see your students doing as (readers, writers, mathematicians, scientists, etc.)?
4. Is there any student work or data that could help us decide on a focus that would make the most impact on your students?
5. How do you feel about the goal we've selected? Does it feel right to you?

A FINAL THOUGHT

Landing on a meaningful goal involves a combination of understanding the standards, hearing the concerns of the teacher, and creating a plan that is both realistic and inspirational. We avoid making goal setting a bureaucratic process. We prefer to think about goals for coaching cycles as being organic and motivational.

While goal setting drives so much of what we do in life, it is just the beginning. We can think, "I'm going to eat a healthy dinner tonight," "I'm going to watch less TV," or "I'm going to exercise more often," but we need more to truly change our behavior. We need guidance, encouragement, skills, and tools to reach our goals. That's what coaching is about. It's about helping teachers reach their goals for students. We can't stand around and hope that teachers will work hard toward *our* goals. That would be counter to everything we know about motivation and engagement. Rather, we see goal setting as an opportunity. It reminds teachers that we are committed to treating them with respect and, in turn, to creating trusting partnerships. As coaches, we can never forget that our job is to work side by side with teachers to help them reach their goals for student learning. This is how it all begins.

2 Using Learning Targets

Several years ago, Leanna was working with a humanities teacher named Thomas at an alternative high school. As the two started to plan together, Thomas shared, "You know, I get my best ideas for lessons from listening to National Public Radio on the way to work." Thomas was a very deep thinker and had an almost magical ability to engage his students, so on some level he was able to pull this off. Yet, when it came to coaching, it was hard for Leanna to find a way to give the coaching cycle purpose and direction with this as his starting point. She wondered how much more his students would be able to accomplish if he built on his natural talents by being more intentional in his planning and instruction.

Fast forward fifteen years, and you would be hard pressed to find a teacher who is given as much leeway as Thomas was given back then. Today we have standards to guide us regarding what is expected of our students in both content and process. And thanks to the work of educational leaders like Wiggins and McTighe (2005), we understand how to plan backward using these standards. In their seminal book *Understanding by Design*, Wiggins and McTighe write, "We are quick to say what things *we* like to teach, what activities *we* will do, and what kinds of resources *we* will use; but without clarifying the desired results of our teaching, how will we ever know whether our designs are appropriate or arbitrary? How will we distinguish merely interesting learning from *effective* learning? More pointedly, how will we ever meet content standards or arrive at hard-won understandings unless we think through what those goals imply for the learner's activities and achievements?" (p. 14). We agree wholeheartedly and have worked hard to embed this very notion into each and every coaching cycle.

When we use standards to create a set of learning targets, we set a coaching cycle up for success. *Using learning targets* is about grappling with what we think a particular standard really means by discussing the discrete knowledge and skills that are required. These conversations can be challenging and messy, but it is a powerful process of collaboration that leads to a high level of clarity for all parties involved. We owe it to our students to deeply understand and teach into the standards. This coaching move gets us there.

THE MOVE—*USING LEARNING TARGETS*

Once a rigorous, student-centered goal has been set for a coaching cycle, our next step is to break down the goal into a collection of student-friendly learning targets. These learning targets are vital to the success of the coaching cycle because they provide a vision for what students will need to know and be able to do in order to meet the goal. If there are no steps along the way set forth at the outset, the coaching cycle can often feel untethered and lacking direction. When standards-based learning targets are clearly defined at the beginning of the coaching cycle, both the coach and teacher have a road map for the learning opportunities that will be planned over time. Ultimately, these learning targets will provide the criteria by which the teacher, coach, and students will measure their progress toward meeting the goal.

WHY *USING LEARNING TARGETS* IS IMPORTANT

Leanna's friend, Salina, was interested in learning taekwondo and set the ambitious goal of becoming a black belt. Starting as a beginner, Salina embarked on a journey that took her about two years of hard work and perseverance. Taking classes at a nearby dojo for three, and often four times a week, she had to progress through a total of ten belts to finally earn the coveted black belt. At each level, the expectations were clearly articulated by her instructor. Salina understood the skills and techniques that were necessary to master each level, and because of this she was able to receive relevant and targeted feedback every step of the way. She felt this kept her focused and motivated and ultimately enabled her to meet her goal.

Susan Brookhart and Connie Moss (2014) point to a similar phenomenon in education. They write, "When students understand exactly what they're supposed to learn and what their work will look like when they learn it, they're better able to monitor and adjust their work, select effective strategies, and connect current work to prior learning" (p. 28). This reminds us that in addition to providing a clear sense of direction for the coaching cycle, *using learning targets* is a coaching move that will have a powerful impact on student achievement.

Defining the learning targets up front, and then consistently referring to them in the planning and delivery of instruction, the teacher and coach are able to provide opportunities for students to gain a clear understanding of what they need to know and be able to do, take ownership of their learning, and have the criteria by which to measure their progress. This will enable them to meet the goals set forth for them as learners, in much the same way that Salina was able to earn a black belt in taekwondo.

WHAT *USING LEARNING TARGETS* LOOKS LIKE

Some of our most interesting conversations revolve around figuring out what we *really* want the students to know and be able to do. We push ourselves beyond what's on the test to thinking about learning in the truest sense of the word. Often these conversations occur with teams of teachers.

While working with a group of coaches, Diane was asked to model unpacking a standard with a fourth-grade team who was embarking on a coaching cycle around a new unit of study in writing. The unit included an overview and was connected to the standards. What was lacking were student-friendly learning targets.

As a team of coaches observed, Diane worked with the teachers to create a set of learning targets on chart paper. Within a few minutes, the conversation jumped to the teachers sharing ideas about how they would teach the lessons *before* they had established clarity about the learning targets. At this point, Diane suggested that the group keep those ideas in mind because they would be very important after the learning targets were figured out. She explained that, for now, it was important to be clear about what the students should know and be able to do. Then later, the team would be in a better position to plan lessons that were aligned with the standards.

When she debriefed with the coaches, Diane brought up how common it is for teachers to jump to planning lessons before they have developed learning targets. In observing the conversation, the coaches were able to see the value in *using learning targets*. This helped them slow down and take time to gain clarity about the steps it would take for students to meet the goal for the writing unit. Here are some ways to take this coaching move even further.

QR Code 2.1

Creating and Using Learning Targets, Secondary

http://qrs.ly/ij59nuf

Know the Criteria for High Quality Targets

Crafting high-quality learning targets can sometimes feel like trying to juggle tennis balls while walking across a tight rope; it requires skill, balance, and consideration of a number of factors all at once. In the book, *Where Great Teaching Begins*, Anne Reeves (2011) offers a helpful way to check the validity of a learning target as she suggests that we, "ask whether it is student-centered, is thinking-centered, and describes a performance that demonstrates learning" (p. 70).

When learning targets are student-centered, they focus on how students will demonstrate their new learning. This leads us to ask ourselves how the learning will be measured. In other words, how will the teacher, coach, and students know if the target has been met? Reeves (2011) reminds us that "[i]f the performance is something that's not directly observable—an analysis, for example—the teacher must ensure that it can be readily demonstrated in an observable form, such as in writing or in a graphic organizer" (p. 70). Making learning visible helps us make it measurable.

Academic and intellectual rigor are qualities we strive for in every aspect of teaching. This begins with learning targets. To this end, we are careful not to limit ourselves to targets that only require lower-level thinking skills. While there's certainly a place for attaining basic facts, knowledge, and concepts in all subject areas, we can take steps to ensure that our learning targets ask students to do more of the heavy lifting necessary in higher-order thinking as well. Additionally, the standards remind us that along with the content that the students need to know and interact with, there is also a set of necessary skills for students to learn. Webb's theory of the Depth of Knowledge is a useful framework to refer to in order to ensure that our learning targets cover the spectrum of the levels of thinking that we are after (Figure 2.1).

There is a lot to take into consideration when we are thinking about the types of learning targets that we focus on during our coaching cycles. Along with Reeves's (2011) guidelines, we also need to think about the appropriate size and scope of learning targets. We have to watch out for targets that are too broad in content or concept, for example, "I can describe all the key factors that led up to World War I," or "I can explain volume formulas and use them to solve problems." On the other end of the spectrum, we don't want targets that can be met within just a few minutes of a class period, such as, "I can write an equation with three operations." Our goal is to craft "just right" targets that are specific and focused in what they require of students, yet meaty enough that they can be worked on for at least a whole class period.

Figure 2.1 Examples of Learning Targets Classified by Webb's Depth of Knowledge

DOK 1	DOK 2	DOK 3	DOK 4
I can identify the characters in the story.	I can predict what might happen next in the story.	I can analyze the crafting techniques that the author used to create a compelling story.	I can write a story that is inspired by crafting techniques and that is compelling to my readers.
I can define common terms that refer to igneous rocks (intrusive, extrusive, hypabyssal, etc.)	I can classify rocks based on a variety of factors.	I can investigate how different types of rocks have developed their unique features.	I can design an experiment that demonstrates my understanding of igneous rocks.

Start by Unpacking the Standard

Our first step in creating a set of targets is to go directly to the source to break down or unpack the standard, just like Diane did with the teachers in the previous example. Since our goals for coaching cycles are standards based, then it makes sense that the learning targets are derived from the standards as well. Grappling to unpack a standard provides a powerful way to go beyond the surface and think deeply about outcomes for students.

Leanna got to observe this first hand when working with Kendra, a middle school coach, as she partnered with a sixth-grade team of math teachers. Their district curriculum department had created a set of learning targets that corresponded with various units of study. Kendra suggested that to truly understand the standards, they should unpack them on their own. When they were looking at the standards for unit rate, Mario said, "I just write 'I can' in front of each section of the standard and have my targets ready to go." He looked at the group with an expression that seemed to say, "If it's this easy, then what's the big fuss about?" But his teammate, Kristen, pushed back. "I've taught this stuff for a few years now, and I'm not even sure I get what it all means. What is it that our students *really* need to know?" Kendra jumped at this opening and recommended that before they got to the actual learning targets, they should start with that exact question: "What is important to know about unit rate?" They decided to look at one of the substandards, "*solve unit rate problems including those involving unit pricing and constant speed.*" What ensued was a complex and engaging dialogue around what the

**QR Code 2.2
Creating Learning Targets With a Fifth-Grade Team**

http://qrs.ly/z359nuk

students needed to know and understand. Here are the ideas the group came up with:

- Unit rate is the constant of proportionality.
- The numbers co-vary.
- You use it to budget and be a savvy consumer.
- It helps you to get the more efficient value.
- It is the constant relationship between two quantities or units.
- It helps you compare.
- Values are equivalent, even though not equally efficient.

Having taken the time to really think through the standard, they were able to develop student-friendly learning targets. These included the following items:

- I can use models to justify equivalence in unit rates.
- I can understand proportional relationships in a variety of contexts.
- I can find unit rate and explain why it's important in real life.
- I can describe the proportional relationship between two quantities using unit rate.
- I can use unit rate to make decisions in real-world situations.

Without Kendra coaching the group, asking probing questions, and continually referring back to the standard, they may not have stayed on track. And as they began to look at the standards in a new light, Mario professed, "There's so much more to most standards than what you see on the surface!" In the end, they were excited to teach into the learning targets that they designed. They also knew that they would continue to re-examine them along the way to see if any tweaking needed to be done. At the end of the meeting, Kristen said, "This is one of the best conversations I've ever had about math. I have a totally new understanding of what and how I need to teach."

Unpacking standards can take place with an individual teacher or a grade-level team, as was the case with Kendra. In whatever form, taking the time to collaborate about what is most important and how these big ideas are represented in the standards helps us develop a deep and true understanding of what students are being asked to learn. Figure 2.2 provides some language stems for these types of conversations.

Align Assessments to Learning Targets

In addition to keeping our coaching work focused on the goal for student learning, *using learning targets* helps us to align our assessments as well. This became evident when Ian was coaching Sue, a high school chemistry teacher, on a tenth-grade unit on matter and energy. Their goal

Figure 2.2 Language Stems for Unpacking Standards

- What do we want the students to know and be able to do?
- What do we want the students to understand?
- What do we mean when we say the students will understand . . . ?
- How might the students demonstrate understanding?
- How can we be sure that we are thinking beyond lessons and activities?
- If we are unsure, it can be helpful to refer to the standard.
- Can you tell us more about what you are thinking?

was this: "Students will know and understand common properties, forms, and changes in matter and energy," and they created a list of learning targets that included the following:

- I can compare and contrast physical and chemical changes.
- I can demonstrate the physical and chemical methods used to separate mixtures that are based on the properties of the substances.
- I can determine the atomic number and mass number of isotopes.
- I can calculate the average atomic mass of an element.

Sue came to their planning session with a test from the textbook that she figured they could use to pre-assess the students. But when they compared Sue's test questions with the learning targets, they found several mismatches between what they identified the students needed to know and be able to do and what the test was asking of them. So they went through each question and decided whether or not it fit with the learning targets. First, they deleted questions that were outside the scope of their targets. Then they created new questions related to targets that were not initially covered in the test. This rich process caused them to look carefully at each question and really think about its purpose. Had they not been equipped with a clear set of learning targets, the mismatch probably wouldn't have come to light until they found themselves with a pile of data that didn't tell them what they really wanted to know. This was such a powerful learning experience for both Sue and Ian, and from then on, Sue never gave an assessment without aligning it to the learning targets first.

Sue and Ian were lucky to have the ability to revise her assessment. Oftentimes, teachers are required to use district assessments and aren't afforded such flexibility. When this is the case it's helpful to switch around the process—instead of aligning the assessment to the targets, we need to be sure that our targets cover everything that is to be assessed. Then we can always add on any targets that aren't addressed in the district test and assess those separately.

Consider Learning Targets as Compared to Rubrics

If you have been accustomed to using rubrics, you may be wondering how they relate to learning targets. You may even question whether you need learning targets if you have a well-designed rubric already in place. These are good points to consider. Rubrics and learning targets are not mutually exclusive. Both provide ways for teachers and students to assess their work. Both, when done well, outline a clear set of criteria for what it looks like to meet a certain level of accomplishment. The main difference is that rubrics are often designed to assess a project or product, whereas learning targets are about naming the learning and thinking we are asking students to do. Learning targets also focus our attention on what *proficiency* looks like. Taken one at a time, the targets show us what it looks like to meet the short-term objective, usually over one to three class periods. As a collection, they show us the success criteria of the bigger goal.

During a recent coaching cycle, Katey and Mary Beth were focusing on analyzing the role of a key figure within the Civil Rights movement. The students would create a research project as the culminating performance assessment for Mary Beth's eighth graders. Since they wanted to track progress on the learning targets throughout the unit *and* have a way to assess the paper, they created a rubric that would accomplish both of these things.

As you read Figure 2.3, you'll notice that Katey and Mary Beth's starting point was identifying the learning targets. Next they moved on to

Figure 2.3 Self-Evaluation Rubric From a Civil Rights Writing Project

Goal: *Students will analyze the role of a key figure within the Civil Rights Movement.*

Learning Target	Exemplary	Accomplished	Not Yet
I can identify the ways in which my person gained power or affected social change in America.		• Describe the dream of my person. • Describe specific actions taken by my person in the Civil Rights Movement. • Give specific examples of the methods my person used to affect change or gain power.	
I can analyze the reasons why my person chose a certain method of social change (violence, nonviolence, etc.).		• Identify the influences that led my person to choose certain methods of social change (family, mentors, life experiences, etc.). • Analyze how these influences affected the actions of my person.	

Learning Target	Exemplary	Accomplished	Not Yet
I can evaluate the effectiveness of how my person gained power or affected social change.		• Provide specific examples of how my person's actions affected his or her dream. • Evaluate specific actions to determine if they were successes or failures. • Describe my person's legacy: What did he or she leave behind? How did he or she affect society?	
I can express my thinking in the form of a research paper.		• Organize my paper around the central and supporting ideas of my research. • Write in a way that is clear and easy for the reader to understand. • Cite evidence that supports my claims. • Use appropriate spelling and conventions.	

think about how the students would reach the targets. This was developed as the instruction unfolded. This way the students could build their understanding of what it would take to reach the learning targets one step at a time.

The ultimate goal was for each student to reach the accomplished level, yet if the students (or teacher) believed they had either exceeded the expectation or fallen short, they could use the space in the empty boxes to indicate how they think they demonstrated the learning target. This provided students with clearly defined and rigorous expectations and some flexibility and openness regarding how they might tackle the project.

LESSONS FROM THE FIELD

It was Lori's fifth year of teaching first- and second-grade students with autism in a self-contained classroom. She came to teaching after spending many years working with children with developmental disabilities in other areas, like vocational and life-skills training. Not having gone through a traditional educator-training program, Lori felt that there were some gaps in her teaching skills, particularly in

(Continued)

(Continued)

the area of writing. She had been doing a good job of teaching her students how to accomplish the basic functions of writing: forming all of the letters correctly, writing words that sit correctly on the line, and some basic grammatical conventions. However, she felt stuck with how to help her students use writing as a means of communicating ideas. In some ways, Lori even questioned whether or not they were capable of moving beyond the basic skills. Either way, she knew she needed to learn more. So she decided to seek out the help of Amy, her school's instructional coach.

Since most of Lori's students were fascinated with the nonfiction books she had in her classroom, it was an easy decision for her to choose informational writing as the focus of her work with Amy. They set the goal, "Students will write an informational piece of text," as a starting point for their coaching cycle. Lori still couldn't envision what this might look like for her students, but, so far, the goal didn't seem totally out of the realm of possibility. Then Amy suggested they look at the first- and second-grade writing standards to determine some learning targets. The first-grade standard requires students to *"Write informative/explanatory texts in which they name a topic, supply some facts about the topic, and provide some sense of closure."* For second grade, the standard is slightly more nuanced, asking students to *"Write informative/explanatory texts in which they introduce a topic, use facts and definitions to develop points, and provide a concluding statement or section."* Topic? Supporting facts? Concluding statement? At this point, Lori admitted she couldn't imagine how she could possibly get her special education students to accomplish something like this.

As a coach, Amy knew she had to help Lori understand how to break the standard down into discreet steps so she could create a vision of what it would take to teach her students to do this kind of writing. Then they would have to make it transparent to the students as well. While Lori was nervous about this, Amy said, "The good thing about targets is that they are designed to be in very concrete, kid-friendly language. This is going to work really well with the kids in your classroom." After lots of discussion, the following are the learning targets that they came up with:

- I can choose a topic to write about and name it in my piece.
- I can include facts about the topic in my writing piece.
- I can write an ending to my piece to show the reader it is finished.

Lori also wanted to integrate the work they had already started with conventions, so they referred to the language standards and added three more targets:

- I can use a capital letter to start each sentence.
- I can use punctuation at the end of each sentence.
- I can use the word wall to spell words correctly in my piece.

Looking over the learning targets, Lori started to feel a bit more optimistic. Amy assured her that the targets would guide them in designing instruction and assessing students along the way. This would allow them to make any needed adjustments.

Next Amy suggested that they pre-assess the students to collect some information about where they were starting. To do this, Lori read aloud a few nonfiction books to the students and then asked them to choose a topic of their own to write about. Figure 2.4 provides an example written by Nathan. This simple assessment gave Lori and Amy the baseline data they were looking for. Then they were ready to use the learning targets within their daily instruction.

Figure 2.4 Nathan's Pre-Assessment

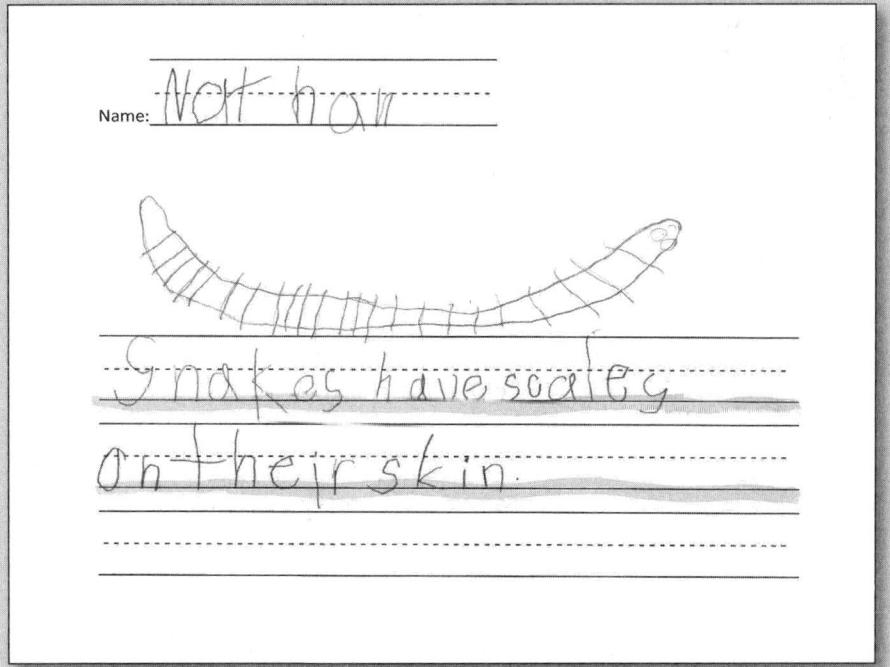

(Continued)

(Continued)

As the coaching cycle progressed, Lori and Amy met on a weekly basis to co-plan lessons that they then taught together. During these co-planning sessions, they first compared the students' writing with the learning targets, then they decided what to do instructionally.

The coaching cycle took place over a five-week period of time. As their work together came to a close, Lori and Amy decided that they were ready see what the students could do on their own. They decided to post-assess much in the same way as they did their pre-assessment. They asked the students to write a piece about a topic they knew about. This way they could assess how the students performed in relation to the learning targets. They were astonished by what the students were able to accomplish (for more on post-assessment of coaching cycles, read Chapter 9).

Figure 2.5 provides Nathan's post-assessment. You'll notice that his writing aligned beautifully with the learning targets. He chose a topic,

Figure 2.5 Nathan's Post-Assessment

CHAPTER 2: Using Learning Targets • 37

(Continued)

(Continued)

provided facts, and included an ending. He even demonstrated the ability to use capital letters, periods, and correctly spell common words. As she reflected back on the coaching cycle, Lori said, "Having the learning targets really helped me see what we were going to be doing with the kids, and they kept us all on track. And they did better than they have ever done as writers." We'd argue that much of their success was based on having clear, student-friendly learning targets to work toward.

TOOLS AND TECHNIQUES

Troubleshooting Learning Targets

It can take some time for teachers to get used to *using learning targets* as part of a coaching cycle. In the past, coaching often focused squarely on what we want teachers to do differently in their classrooms, so moving the conversation to student outcomes may be a bit of a shift. The language in Figure 2.6 provides a clear purpose and rationale for using this coaching move.

Figure 2.6 Language for Using Learning Targets

If I hear . . .	Then I can use the following language . . .
I know I'm supposed to teach to the standards, but I can't see how my kids will be able to do all that.	Let's take a look at the standards that we're going for and break them down to a set of clear learning targets. This will be our road map to get your students from where they are now to where we want them to be.
I have so much content to cover in this unit. I just don't know that I have time for learning targets, too.	I understand that there is a lot of content your students need to know. Let's also think about the type of thinking we want them to be doing around the content and create a set of targets that addresses both components of their learning.
Our district already has learning targets. Can't we just use those?	Let's use the targets we already have as a starting point. It's helpful to review what's there and decide if they align with what we are trying to accomplish. We may even unpack them further or add in something that's missing. They will guide us throughout the coaching cycle, so we want to be sure they are just right.

Guiding Questions for Crafting Learning Targets

The following questions are a helpful guide for coaches who are just getting used to working with teachers to establish student-friendly learning targets. We recommend engaging in these conversations even if the district provides learning targets as a feature of their curriculum. Clarity is everything when it comes to teaching into student outcomes, and conversations among teachers and coaches are the best way to get there (see Figure 2.7).

Figure 2.7 Guiding Questions for Crafting Learning Targets

When thinking about learning targets, we ask ourselves the following guiding questions:

- Is the target directly related to our goal for the coaching cycle and the standard(s) that support it?
- Is the target written in kid-friendly language?
- Does the target focus on learning rather than on a task or activity?
- Can this target be measured?
- Is the target "just right" in size? Does it contain only one action or piece of content?
- Is there a balance of knowledge, reasoning, and skills across a set of learning targets?

Co-Planning With Learning Targets in Mind

Learning targets inform every step of the way in a coaching cycle. Figure 2.8 provides an example of how a teacher and coach integrate learning targets into a co-planning session.

Figure 2.8 Co-Planning With Learning Targets

Learning Target for Today's Lesson:		
I can include facts about the topic in my writing piece.		
	Plan for the Lesson	**How We Will Formatively Assess**
Mini Lesson	• Post the learning target, "I can include facts about the topic in my writing piece." Talk about how this is essential for nonfiction writing.	Students will do a turn and talk at certain points as the mentor text is read aloud. The teacher will also do some thinking aloud. The whole book won't be read,

(Continued)

Figure 2.8 (Continued)

	Learning Target for Today's Lesson: I can include facts about the topic in my writing piece.	
	Plan for the Lesson	**How We Will Formatively Assess**
	• Use a mentor text about octopus to show how the author included facts. Point out that facts are often interesting and surprising, for example, "An octopus can unscrew a lid from a jar. This shows that they are intelligent and can use their hands to get at prey." • Send the students off to try to add facts to their own writing.	rather the teacher will read selected pages that have good examples of facts. Each time the students encounter a fact, they will talk with a partner about what they noticed. As they share, the teacher and coach will listen in to student discussions.
Writing Time	• Some students will write independently. • The teacher and coach will lead an invitational small group for students who need extra support. They will refer to the learning target if students are forgetting to include facts.	Students will work on adding facts to their own writing. This writing will be analyzed in the next co-planning session. If they don't know any facts to add, the students will be encouraged to join the invitational group.
Share Session	• The teacher and coach will identify students to share. Students will be selected based on how they approached the learning target. In this way, the learning target will be revisited, and the students will be provided with more models for how to get there.	Students listen to examples of how facts were added to other students' pieces of writing. As the lesson wraps up, the students share how they will continue to work toward this learning target.

Protocol for Unpacking Standards

A protocol can be a useful tool for unpacking standards with groups of teachers. The following protocol adapted from Stiggins, Arter, Chappuis, and Chappuis (2006, p. 64) is designed to be both open ended and structured. This will ensure that the conversation leads to a great set of learning targets (see Figure 2.9).

Figure 2.9 *Protocol for Unpacking Standards Based on Knowledge, Reasoning, and Skills*

1. Once a goal for the coaching cycle has been determined, refer to the standard or standards that will be addressed. Pose the question, "What will students need to know and be able to do in order to meet this goal?"
2. In answering the question, create a list of potential learning targets.
3. Go through the list of targets one by one, asking the following questions:

   - Does this target represent factual or procedural knowledge that is to be acquired? (Knowledge)
   - Does this target require the skillful use or application of knowledge? (Reasoning)
   - Does this target address a performance that must be demonstrated in order to be observed or assessed? (Skill)

4. Use the word bank along with these questions to help you categorize and refine the list of targets.

Knowledge	Reasoning	Skill
Explain, understand, describe, identify, name, tell, define, recall, match, know, recognize, label	Analyze, compare/contrast, synthesize, classify, infer/deduce, evaluate, interpret	Listen, perform, conduct, read, speak, assemble, operate, measure, model, use, conduct

A FINAL THOUGHT

Using learning targets is a high-leverage coaching move that has a big impact on teacher practice and student achievement. As we think about coaching moves we can use at the beginning of a cycle, it is easy to see how *using learning targets* helps create a pathway, or road map, to guide teaching and learning toward a goal for students. Much like Salina found that clear expectations kept her focused and enabled her to get targeted feedback at every step in her quest for a black belt, learning targets constitute a vital component of virtually *every* aspect of the cycle, beyond just the initial planning phase. We use them to design and align meaningful pre-assessments, they direct our daily and weekly planning, teachers and students access them throughout a lesson for on-the-spot checks for understanding, and we assess with targets in mind to adjust and differentiate instruction. Finally, they are the success criteria by which students, teachers, and coaches can determine whether or not the goal has been met at the end of the coaching cycle. It is hard to overstate the power and importance of *using learning* targets. If we fail to start a coaching cycle with a well-crafted set of targets, we will miss out on all of the subsequent opportunities to use them along the way.

3 Getting Ready for Coaching in the Classroom

Classrooms are like laboratories. While scientists look closely at natural occurrences and then work to understand them on a deeper level, teachers analyze student evidence to create the best conditions for learning. Scientists have successfully landed a rover on Mars, have monitored the impact of global warming on animal populations, and have developed life-saving vaccines. We'd all agree that this is complex work. Yet the work that teachers do in classrooms is equally as complex and demands the same level of analysis and reflection.

As we observe student learning, we seek to understand where the students are on a continual basis by asking, "How are my students engaging as learners? Is anyone confused? How deep are they going in their thinking? Am I noticing any misconceptions? What about my advanced learners—are they being challenged?" What we thought of as a lesson becomes an incredibly complex experiment in moving an entire classroom of learners forward. Given this complexity, how can we expect teachers to accomplish this alone? The job is far too important to expect that. Rather, we can provide teachers with coaching that helps them reach their goals for students by working side by side while teaching and learning occurs.

THE MOVE—*GETTING READY FOR COACHING IN THE CLASSROOM*

In the 1990s, Cook and Friend (1995) introduced the concept of co-teaching in their work on inclusion in special education. This provided a new paradigm for partnering while delivering instruction. At the time, having two teachers in a classroom was rare, and teachers weren't sure about how to share the teaching load. Today, teachers are finding many opportunities to co-teach, including during coaching cycles. In this chapter, we introduce how we have built upon the work of Cook and Friend and expanded it to create a vision for what a coach might be doing while in the classroom. This vision puts a spin on the traditional definition of co-teaching and puts it squarely within a coaching context.

Even with an understanding of co-teaching in today's schools, applying it to coaching may take some getting used to. Some teachers don't have a sense of what it feels like to teach alongside a coach. Others may prefer to go it alone in their classrooms. And some may jump right in with little hesitation. These different perspectives demonstrate the importance of working thoughtfully with teachers to create the conditions for getting the most out of our time when we are in classrooms. Being intentional about how we will work together in classrooms is how we *get ready for coaching in the classroom.*

WHY *GETTING READY FOR COACHING IN THE CLASSROOM* IS IMPORTANT

Classrooms can feel like private spaces that are off limits to outsiders. As coaches, we may find ourselves lingering on the threshold of classroom doors, unsure about how to proceed. We know that coaching ought to be rigorous and meaningful because teachers are investing their precious time to work with us. Yet, we don't always feel sure about how to work in the classrooms of others. "Should I observe and take notes from the back of the classroom? Should I stay quiet throughout the lesson (even though I might have insights about how the students are doing)? Would it bother the teacher if I spoke up?" This uncertainty creates an obvious barrier to authentic collaboration during a lesson.

In their book *Taking the Lead,* Killion and Harrison (2006) advocate for creating partnership agreements with teachers. They write, "Sharing responsibility for success is the beginning of a mutually satisfying relationship in which both the client and the coach feel connected, responsible, and accountable for the results of the work" (p. 119). Discussing how a teacher and coach will collaborate during a lesson is an important component of a partnership agreement for coaching.

Early in her work as a literacy coach, Diane was beginning a coaching cycle with a third-grade teacher. Unaware of partnership agreements, Diane jumped from the invitation to work with Rhonda straight into her classroom on the first day of the cycle. She figured that they were friendly, and even shared some interests outside of school, so what could go wrong?

When she arrived on the first day of the coaching cycle, it became apparent that co-teaching was not what Rhonda had in mind. She met Diane at the classroom door, pointed to a large set of wooden cubbies, and said, "Right here, I have cubbies set up for my students. I wanted to let you know that I made a cubby for you, too. I'll put the papers there for you to use with your small group, and then you can put them back when you leave. Here's a list of the students you will be working with." Diane wasn't sure what to say. It seemed as if she was expected to go off in the corner and teach a small group of students. She wondered how coaching would happen under these circumstances.

As she stood there with a stack of papers in her hand, Diane wished she could press rewind and talk with Rhonda about what their partnership would look like. She considered settling in at the back table to work with the small group for the next few weeks, call it a coaching cycle, and then move on. This felt safer than nudging Rhonda in a direction that she didn't seem interested in going. Or, she could sit down with Rhonda to reframe the purpose for a coaching cycle. This felt like a riskier option. But after giving it some thought, Diane decided to at least try to salvage the coaching cycle by recommending other ways they might work together, including co-planning and co-teaching.

Having this conversation wasn't easy, particularly since the coaching cycle had already begun. When Diane brought up the option of co-teaching, Rhonda seemed unsure. So Diane suggested, "How about if we plan and then teach some of the lessons together?" After thinking it through, Rhonda agreed to give it a try. And as their work shifted to more of a partnership, the cubby went unused. But even with these positive steps, Diane couldn't help but notice that the coaching cycle felt strained. She suspected that Rhonda had hoped that she would work with one specific group of struggling students, and when she reframed her role as a coach, Rhonda may have felt that she wasn't getting what she had signed up for.

This experience provided an invaluable lesson about setting agreements *before* a coaching cycle rather than working from assumptions about what we think will happen. If a coaching cycle is built on a shaky foundation, it almost always feels strained. And when coaching cycles feel strained, we diminish our ability to impact student learning.

WHAT *GETTING READY FOR COACHING IN THE CLASSROOM* LOOKS LIKE

There are a variety of ways to approach *getting ready for coaching in the classroom.* After working with the teacher to set a goal for student learning, the coach may simply ask how the teacher would like to collaborate while in the classroom. Or the coach may provide the teacher with a menu of options for coaching in the classroom (see Figure 3.1). The key is to get on the same page with teachers before the door to the classroom even opens.

Choice is as important for adult learners as it is for our students. Planning what it will look like is an opportunity to build choice into our collegial relationships with teachers. In certain situations, these norm-setting conversations may take on an organic tone wherein the teacher and coach naturally engage in a discussion about what their partnerships will look like. Other times, it may be helpful to introduce options so that teachers can more easily envision what their partnership will look like when the coach comes to their classroom. Several of these coaching moves will be detailed in upcoming chapters.

Figure 3.1 Options for Coaching in the Classroom

Coaching Move	What It Looks Like
Noticing and Naming	During the lesson, the teacher and coach focus on how the students are demonstrating their current understanding in relation to the learning targets. As we work with students, we will record student evidence that we will use in our planning conversations.
Thinking Aloud	The teacher and coach share their thinking throughout the delivery of a lesson. By being metacognitive in this way, we will be able to name successes and work through challenges in real time.
Teaching in Tandem	The teacher and coach work together to co-deliver the lesson. The lesson is co-planned to ensure that our roles are clear, the learning targets are defined, and we both understand how the lesson is crafted.
Co-Conferring	The teacher and coach sit side by side when conferring with students. This way they create a shared understanding of how the students are doing. This then informs the next lesson.
You Pick Four	The teacher identifies approximately four students who the coach will pay special attention to in order to collect student evidence. The coach keeps the learning targets in mind while collecting student evidence. This evidence is then used in future planning conversations.
Micro Modeling	A *portion* of the lesson is modeled by the coach. The teacher and coach base their decision about what is modeled on the needs that have been identified by the teacher. Micro modeling may occur during a whole group lesson, conference, small group, or so on.

Think Beyond Co-Delivering Instruction

When we suggest the idea of co-teaching to secondary coaches, they often wonder how they will possibly take an active role in content-rich classes. These classes demand a deep understanding of the subject matter, and they feel it may not make sense to co-teach in a class like AP statistics or art history. We recently encountered this question from Tara and Sara, two coaches in large high schools in Missouri. As we shared the notion of coaching in the classroom, we could tell that they were wondering how it would translate to their work in secondary schools.

Their question was timely given the fact that in the afternoon we would be heading over to Sara's school to observe her coaching an eleventh-grade finance teacher. Sara's background was in humanities, and Adrienne was planning to teach a lesson on the stock market that day. Even though it was unfamiliar content, Sara knew that she didn't want to lurk in the back of the class during the lesson. She also knew that co-delivering the lesson wasn't an option. She had to figure out another way to coach while in Adrienne's classroom.

As they sat down to plan the lesson, Sara reminded Adrienne of an earlier conversation when she had mentioned some concerns she was having about a few of her students. Sara used this as an opening and suggested that she could spend the class period collecting student evidence about how these specific students did throughout the lesson. Then they could use the student evidence during their planning conversation. Adrienne liked Sara's idea because with such a large class, she wasn't always able to collect evidence on every one of her students. She was worried about how they were progressing and liked the idea of someone spending the class period watching for this.

Adrienne provided Sara with the names of four students and shared some background about how she hoped they would engage as learners. Rather than teaching the students who were identified, Sara's role would be to observe, confer with, and collect student evidence. With this simple step, they were ready to work together—even in a content-rich classroom. Since then, we have named Sara's coaching move *"you pick four"* and have used it in K–12 classrooms across all content areas.

Increase Co-Teaching, Decrease Modeling and Observation

Imagine you hired a tennis coach to help you improve your game. Then you showed up for the first lesson, and he suggested that you

QR Code 3.1
Getting Ready for a Coaching Cycle With a Sixth-Grade Team

http://qrs.ly/7s59num

observe as he played for the next hour. You'd probably ask for your money back. What if he suggested that he spend the hour observing you? He'll take some notes, and then the two of you will go through it in a few days. Again, you'd be wondering why you are paying this guy. What if he suggested that you focus on your game, and since you are so busy, he will help you out by picking up your balls? You would be wondering when your coach actually planned to provide you with some coaching. By now you may have recognized some of the most common practices used by coaches: modeling, observing, and serving as a resource provider. While each of these methods offer some value to teachers, there are other ways we can take coaching to the next level.

Most of us would define a good coach as someone who helps you get better at your game. Someone who is on the court, by your side, making sure you reach your goals. When we model an entire lesson, it assumes that transfer is as easy as watching and doing. This can lead to an uneven relationship that puts the teacher in a passive role with the coach as the expert. On the other hand, observing teachers may feel more like evaluation than coaching. If your tennis coach took this approach, you'd be anxiously wondering what he *really* thought—if you looked silly or if you were on the right track in your game. Then again, when we serve as resource providers, we are being helpful at the expense of coaching. There is no question that teachers are overwhelmed and busy. But this is all the more reason to get in there and coach the teachers toward their goals for teaching and learning.

While there can be value in modeling lessons or observing teachers, we find that creating a more dynamic interplay between the teacher and coach provides deeper levels of reflection and implementation. We never want to leave teachers wondering what they should be doing. Is the expectation for the teacher to replicate what they just observed at a later time? This can be tricky given the fact that they will be on to a new lesson the following day. Should the teacher compare what they observed with how they typically deliver a lesson? This could send a message that the coach is a better teacher and, in turn, may undermine the partnership that the coach is working so hard to create. We believe that teachers need more. They need a thinking partner throughout a lesson so that they can work through their delivery with a *guide on the side*. This is what coaching in the classroom is about.

Clarify the Learning Targets

Getting ready for coaching in the classroom includes developing a shared vision for what the students will know and be able to do. These are the learning targets that we introduced in Chapter 2. Without clearly defined expectations for student learning, we are less able to partner with teachers to get students where they need to be. With well-established learning targets, we are on the same page and able to reflect and adjust our teaching throughout the lesson.

In addition to impacting the delivery of the lesson, clearly articulated learning targets affect how we plan together. If we don't have a clear vision for what the students should know and be able to do, then planning becomes vague and less connected to student learning. This decreases our ability to adjust our instruction in a way that moves student learning forward. It also makes it difficult to pinpoint how we will use effective instructional practices in a student-centered manner. When we have clearly articulated learning targets, we are able to link our instructional decision making to student learning. We do this by asking questions like "How did the students do in relation to the learning targets?" And "What should we do in the next lesson to move the students further?" Clearly articulated learning targets make these conversations possible.

Define How You Will Co-Plan

Being intentional about we will co-plan helps us avoid the awkward moment that comes when we pop into the classroom when a lesson is taking place. If our goal is to think with teachers about which instructional moves will have the greatest effect on student learning, then we need to sit down together and co-plan lessons on a regular basis. In this way, we develop clarity around how instruction will progress and how the teacher and coach will share the responsibility for the lesson. This may sound time intensive to a busy teacher, so we like to keep it simple. While we make sure to co-plan the lessons that we will teach together, we may even rough out the plans for a whole week's worth of instruction. Approaching these conversations through a series of reflective questions, like those in Figure 3.2, keeps the conversation on track and focused.

Figure 3.2 Questions for Co-Planning

- What is the learning target for the lesson?
- How do we think the students will demonstrate their learning (in writing, verbally)?
- How will new content be delivered and by who?
- How will we formatively assess students?
- What resources, materials, or technology will we need to get ready?
- How will we work together to manage student behavior?

Be Okay With Slowing Down

We find that much of our coaching work involves slowing down the pace of instruction. While teachers know that formative assessment, providing opportunities for discourse and dialogue, differentiating instruction, and providing feedback to students are effective practices to use in the classroom, they sometimes feel too rushed to do these things. Rather, they march through the pacing guide, teach the lessons, and hope that the students will learn. With so much pressure on plowing forward, it is hard for teachers to give themselves the permission to slow down.

For this reason, coaching cycles may serve as a way to slow down instruction. This way the coach and teacher are able to spend the time they need to analyze student learning and adjust the instruction to meet their needs. This means that the teacher may not stay on pace with other teachers in the department or grade level. We have found that in certain teams, this can put the participating teacher under some degree of stress because the other teachers may take more of a lock-step approach and may pressure the participating teacher to do the same. Therefore, we recommend having a conversation about the pacing of instruction throughout a coaching cycle. For example, the coach may say, "We are going to be working hard to meet your students' needs. That means we will be guided by the learning targets and formative assessments, and we may get off pace from the rest of your team. But you can be assured that your students will be learning." Being clear on what to expect for the teacher and sharing it with his or her team and even the principal are ways to ensure that slowing down becomes a positive part of the coaching work, rather than a source of stress and anxiety.

Plan How You Will Collect Evidence While in the Classroom

Before diving into coaching in the classroom, it is helpful to discuss how the teacher and coach will collect student evidence. In *Student-Centered Coaching*, Diane (Sweeney, 2011) shared how her note-taking has changed as her coaching has evolved. She wrote, "In the past, I used a two-column note-taking format where I wrote my questions and ideas on one side and a description of the lesson on the other. In the debriefing session, I shared my thinking and ideas with the teacher and assumed that he or she would run off to use the myriad of brilliant teaching strategies that I suggested. Now, when I spend time in the classroom, the lens is on the students. I focus my attention on collecting evidence about what the students do using a note-taking tool that is designed for this purpose," (p. 20).

Amber recently used this note-taking strategy when working with teachers in an international school in Santiago, Chile. She was coaching a first-grade teacher, and it was the third day of school. The learning target was "I can put my stories on paper in pictures and/or words," a great target for the first few days of first grade because it aligned directly with both the standards and their writing curriculum. It was also specific enough to collect a solid body of student evidence while in the classroom.

As they prepared for the lesson, Amber provided options for how they could partner during instruction. Pamela chose *teaching in tandem* and *noticing and naming* as the co-teaching moves she would like to try during the lesson. She also created a note-taking grid so that they would both be able to collect evidence as they worked with students (see Figure 3.3). Taking notes in this way eased any discomfort that Pamela may have had because she quickly understood that coaching was about how her students were doing as writers, instead of how she did in the delivery of her lesson.

As Amber listened to the students and recorded her notes, it became apparent that they were confident, able to take risks, and happily willing

QR Code 3.2

Setting Norms for a Coaching Cycle With a First-Grade Team

http://qrs.ly/6w59nur

Figure 3.3 Notes From Pamela's Class

Learning target: *I can put my stories on paper in pictures and/or words.*

1. Marco Wrote a lot of words	2. Julio Drew pictures	3. Marie Put name on paper and then sat and thought; later, began to draw	4. Lee Pictures and words	5. Geraldo Detailed drawing and words to match
6. Timothy Jumps right to drawing a detailed picture	7. Sonny Pictures and words	8. Spencer His idea—about falling down a slide; writing words and pictures	9. Jack Detailed drawing, then went back to add words	10. Susanna Seems stuck. Lots of erasing. She got going after a few minutes and drew a picture.

(Continued)

Figure 3.3 (Continued)

11. Marcus Words and pictures	12. Maggie Words and pictures, wrote across three pages	13. Salvador Wrote words across the three pages.	14. Julio Started with a picture, added words, went back to add to the picture.	15. Jose Jumps right to drawing a detailed picture
16. Agustin Suggested in conference he draw himself to get started. This gets him going.	17. Dylan Fully developed writing with no picture. Confer and suggest he draw a picture to go with his words.	18. Tika Draws a bus, gives to assistant. Assistant redirects. Draws a bus on page two.		

to get their ideas down in pictures and words. And because the observations focused on what students *can* do instead of what they cannot, Pamela was pleasantly surprised as well. She couldn't wait to talk more about what she would do tomorrow to build on what her students did today. They ultimately decided to rethink some of the lessons they thought they would teach in the following few days, agreeing that there was no point in teaching what the students already knew. This is a wonderful example of how student-centered coaching is driven by how the students are performing on any given day. In this case, the coach and teacher didn't need to slow down instruction, they were able to speed it up.

LESSONS FROM THE FIELD

In a recent project, Leanna had the opportunity to work with Robert, a new coach at a high school in New York. When they first met, Leanna had no doubt that Robert had the disposition of a coach. He was kind, a good listener, and understood how to engage his students as learners.

He was about three months into his job when they sat down for their first problem-solving session. Leanna began by asking how he was feeling about getting his coaching up and running. He looked a little bit sheepish and said, "That's something I've been wanting to pick your brain about. To be honest, I'm having a hard time making inroads with certain teachers. They seem standoffish, and when I do get into their classrooms, they don't seem very engaged. I'm not sure what I'm doing wrong."

As she listened, Leanna suspected that Robert's challenges might have something to do with the coaching practices that he was using. She asked, "Can you tell me how you have been spending your time as a coach?" Robert responded, "Mostly I am going into classrooms and observing teachers. Then we sit down afterward to debrief. During the debriefing session, I usually celebrate what's going well, and then I give the teacher feedback about what they could do differently next time."

Leanna wondered if Robert's observations were affecting his ability to forge partnerships with teachers. While she was certain that he had a kind and generous soul, she suspected that he had diminished these qualities by limiting his coaching practice to observation. She pointed out that, while it wasn't his intention, this choice may have put him in the role of evaluator. She suggested, "What if you decreased your time observing teachers and increased the time you spent working in partnership while in the classroom? It seems that this is what teachers will really need if they are going to reflect and grow in their practice." As he thought about what Leanna was suggesting, Robert began to understand how the teachers perceived him. While he viewed himself as a partner, his actions weren't necessarily matching that vision.

As they worked together to shift Robert's coaching practice to include less observing, he pointed out that an important first step would be to communicate his plan with the principal and teachers. He felt that if he had support from leadership, then he would be able to adjust how he had been going about his coaching. After that, he would work with teachers to consider options. He didn't want to step on anyone's toes, so he thought he'd get their input regarding what it might look like.

(Continued)

(Continued)

Leanna helped Robert draft a letter to teachers that framed his new vision for coaching (see Figure 3.4). By sharing his thinking with teachers in an open and honest way, he hoped that the teachers would see him in a new light and that this would create more meaningful opportunities for how they could work together. His goal was to work individually with teachers to help them figure out what they wanted coaching in the classroom to look like. To accomplish this, Robert would refer to the options that were included in Figure 3.1 so that the teachers would better understand and be actively involved in his coaching. But first, he wanted to begin moving away from the role of observer. He knew that shifting his approach would take time, but he felt that working side by side with teachers would make a big difference in how he was perceived throughout his school.

Figure 3.4 Robert's Letter to Teachers

Dear Friends,

As many of you know, I have been on a steep learning curve as an instructional coach at WHS. One of my favorite parts of the job has been spending time with each of you in your classrooms. It has been a rare treat to get to know all of the students in our school. I am also struck by the unique qualities that each of you bring to your teaching. It has been a gift to get to know each of you.

As we move into the second quarter, I am thinking about how I might improve my coaching. The time I've spent observing in classrooms has provided wonderful opportunities to learn from you and your students. Yet I feel it is limiting our ability to work together to increase student learning. Lately, I have been wondering if you might have felt the same way.

In the next few weeks, I'd like to check in with you to discuss how we might work together while I am in your classroom. While I have a few ideas, I'm sure you do as well. I think by brainstorming a bit, we will figure out a way to work together that meets both your and your students' needs. Thank you for your patience with me as a coach. I look forward to continuing our learning journey.

Warmly,

Robert

When Leanna checked in with Robert a few months later, he reported that he was working in more and more classrooms. He explained that his coaching felt much more natural, and teachers seemed to be more engaged. He was hearing that some teachers still wanted to be observed so that they could receive direct feedback on their teaching. And from time to time, he found himself modeling a lesson. But mostly, he was finding that co-teaching was his most valuable coaching move.

TOOLS AND TECHNIQUES

Troubleshooting Conversations Around Getting Ready for Coaching in the Classroom

Discussing how a teacher and coach will share a lesson can feel awkward. Sometimes it feels as if we are overstepping our bounds, or we may fear that the teacher has a different vision for coaching altogether. Figure 3.5 provides an if/then chart to help coaches troubleshoot their discussions about coaching in the classroom.

Figure 3.5 Language for Getting Ready for Coaching in the Classroom

If I hear . . .	Then I can use the following language . . .
I'd love to see you teach. Would you model it for me?	I'd be happy to model a portion of the lesson. But it may be more beneficial for us to both take part in the lesson. Let's figure out what you'd like to do and what you'd like me to do. That way we can work together.
It sounds like this might take a lot of time, especially the planning piece.	We do have to be on the same page regarding the lesson. But if we have clear learning targets and a rough idea of what you'd like the lesson to look like, then we should be in good shape.
Are you going to observe the lesson? I really like your feedback.	We can definitely build in some observation. But it would be nice if we could work side by side during the lesson. That way, we can address anything that comes up in the moment, rather than waiting to talk about it a few days later.

Crafting Partnership Agreements

We have learned that rather than assuming that we will work side by side with teachers, we need to carefully plan our conversations about what these partnerships will look like. Whether used orally or in writing, the questions in Figure 3.6 help a coach and teacher map out their path to coaching in the classroom.

Figure 3.6 Partnership Agreement for a Coaching Cycle

I. **What Is Our Focus?**
- What is our goal for student learning?
- What are the learning targets that capture what we want the students to know and be able to do?

II. **How Will We Work Together?**
- There are options for how we can work together in your classroom. Let's talk through these options and pick some that feel right to you.
- There are also options for how we can collect student evidence when we are working together in the classroom? How would you like to go about doing this?
- How will we reflect, both individually and collectively, about our work and students' growth?

III. **How Will We Approach Co-Planning?**
- We will need at least thirty-five to forty minutes each week for planning. What time works for you?
- It is helpful to create a planning system that works for you. How would you like to share this information (Google Docs, planning template, etc.)?

A FINAL THOUGHT

Coaching in the classroom requires some degree of audaciousness on the part of the teacher and coach. We bare our souls when we engage as learners, and this demands, as Roland Barth (2007) puts it, "profound levels of risk taking," (p. 214). Yet, when we set ourselves up for co-teaching, we create countless opportunities for reflection. We no longer wish for do-overs because we are on the same page right from the beginning.

Teachers truly are scientists, working day in and day out to better understand how to help their students learn. When we co-teach, we are engaged in our own form of scientific inquiry. We are also able to create authentic partnerships when we work together in classrooms. It is a dynamic process that weaves its way through a lesson. We aren't in the back of the room recording notes about how the lesson went. Nobody sits by passively while the other person does all of the work. Instead, we share the lesson in a way that extends both student and teacher learning.

If coaching is about using student evidence to analyze where they are and then collaborating to deliver instruction that is differentiated and needs based, then it is easy to imagine coaching in the classroom as an essential practice for pushing learning forward.

4 Noticing and Naming

Not too long ago, a local high school in our area had what might be called a *dream team*—a strong basketball squad returning from last season that lost only two seniors and had a few more talented players coming up from junior varsity. Everyone in town was predicting they would win the state championship. But at a game early in the season, a fairly average team from a neighboring high school upset them with an easy 84–67 win. Something was not right. Immediately following the game, the coach sat the boys down and spelled it out for them. "You missed over 50 percent of your free-throw shots. And the zone defense broke down, and they scored six easy baskets in the fourth quarter." With these statistics, the coach was able to pinpoint two very specific areas where the team was struggling, and the next several practices were devoted entirely to drills that addressed these issues. By the next game, the boys were back on track and eventually did go on to win the state championship that year.

While he undoubtedly played a key part in the team's success, the basketball coach was only doing what most sports coaches do all the time: watching carefully and collecting evidence about what the team needs next. *Noticing and naming* is also about collecting and using evidence. It assumes that data about students are right in front of us, and that we can tap into those data to inform our instructional decision making. Without evidence, we are teaching on a hope and a prayer. With it, we know exactly what the students need and can use that information to help them reach the goals that their teachers have set for them.

THE MOVE—*NOTICING AND NAMING*

Noticing and naming is a dynamic process that takes place when a teacher and coach work side by side in the classroom to surface what the students are doing well and where they have potential to grow. *Noticing* happens when a teacher and coach are actively tuned in and looking for evidence of student learning. *Naming* happens in the explicit use of this information, either on the spot or planning after the lesson, to make decisions about what the students need next. For example, the coach and teacher may engage in discussions with a group of students to uncover their thinking, listen in as students discuss their learning with peers, note what the students are independently reading and writing, or all of the above. The key is for the coach and teacher to collect evidence that informs future instructional decision making. Evidence may include observational data, conference notes, short assignments, exit slips, scripted notes from student-led discussions, student reflections on their own learning, or a myriad of other ways wherein we monitor student learning as it happens.

WHY *NOTICING AND NAMING* IS IMPORTANT

The research is clear; feedback and learning go hand in hand (Hattie, 2012; Pollock, 2012; Stiggins, Arter, Chappuis, & Chappuis, 2006). And when you add formative assessment into the mix, teachers are better able to plan and deliver needs-based instruction. In *Classroom Assessment for Student Learning,* the authors distinguish between assessment *for* learning and assessment *of* learning. They write, "Assessments *for* learning happen while learning is still underway. These are the assessments that we conduct throughout teaching and learning to diagnose student needs, plan our next steps in instruction, provide students with feedback they can use to improve the quality of their work, and help students see and feel in control of their journey to success" (Stiggins, Arter, Chappuis, and Chappuis, 2006, p. 31).

Our learners deserve our close attention so that we can make thoughtful decisions about how to move them forward. It's what all strategic coaches do. They *notice, name,* and then *coach.* Imagine a piano student who is playing a section of music too quickly. What will the teacher focus on? Tempo. How about a speech student who looks down too often and fails to connect with the audience? You got it: eye contact. These examples illustrate the importance of using actual student performance to determine future instruction. While this seems like a no-brainer, the reality is we often need help *seeing* what our students are doing well, *understanding* where they have potential to go further, and then *knowing* what to do about it. Many of our school programs and curricula make the assumption that they can predict what students will need to learn. The message to teachers is that if you follow a predetermined sequence of instruction, then the students will perform. If only it were that easy. No curriculum gets it right for every student in every classroom.

WHAT *NOTICING AND NAMING* LOOKS LIKE

We are careful to frame *noticing and naming* through a positive lens. Operating under the assumption that our students can reach mastery with the right support and encouragement allows us to avoid adopting a deficit mindset. If we give up on our learners, or only notice their weaknesses, then we are done for. Instead, we celebrate incremental growth among our students, and we chart a course for moving them further. All of this rests on a belief that our students can (and will) achieve; they just may not be there *yet*. Here's what we keep in mind when we are *noticing and naming*.

Work From a Clear Understanding of the Learning Targets

For *noticing and naming* to be specific and actionable, we need the learning targets to be at our fingertips—a topic we discussed in Chapter 2. Without them we lose our sense of clarity around what we hope our students will know and be able to do, and we will have no idea what to look for when our students are engaged in learning.

A clear understanding of learning targets also helps a coach navigate added value when coaching in less familiar content areas. Diane experienced this when working with Miguel, a middle school technology coach in Bangkok, Thailand. Miguel asked Diane how he might start working more as a student-centered coach and less as a technology coordinator and asked Diane to join him in Matt's robotics class. Let's just say that robotics is not Diane's specialty, and she wasn't all that sure what coaching could look like or how she might help. So she started at the beginning, with the goal for coaching. Miguel explained that he and Matt would be working on the design cycle. Again, this wasn't an area that was familiar to Diane. So she asked, "What standard are you working toward? Can we start there? Then if we unpack the standard into some student-friendly learning targets this

QR Code 4.1

Noticing and Naming During Middle School Lessons

http://qrs.ly/lk59nus

will give us a clear picture of where we are headed." Matt and Miguel agreed to begin with learning targets. They came up with the following list:

- I can break up the problem visually.
- I can develop and explain a step-by-step plan that includes equations, geometry, and measurement.
- I can work with a partner to develop my thinking.
- I can revise my plan to solve the problem.
- I can reflect on how to approach the problem differently based on what I learned.

With the learning targets in place, it was time to begin coaching in earnest. Diane suggested that Matt begin the lesson, and then she and Miguel could *notice and name* with teams of students. They rotated around the classroom and asked the students to explain their plan and how they were going about developing it. While they hoped to see the students breaking up the problem visually to develop a step-by-step plan, it quickly became apparent that the students had a different idea about what they were expected to do. Miguel and Diane both observed that almost all of the groups were creating sketches with little attention to detail. They chatted with Matt about what they had noticed and agreed that the students would need a model for the type of planning that they were expected to do. This experience was a true test of whether Diane had what it took to coach in a robotics classroom. The beauty was that since the learning targets were clear and included both process and content, she was able to identify gaps in student performance right alongside Matt and Miguel.

We have learned that comparing current student performance with a clear set learning of targets takes the conversation to a place of specificity and action (see Figure 4.1). Working from standards-based

Figure 4.1 Closing the Gap

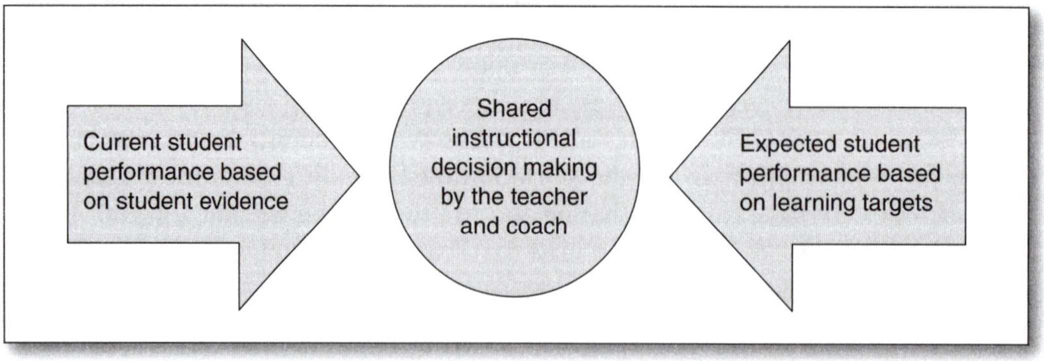

Current student performance based on student evidence → Shared instructional decision making by the teacher and coach ← Expected student performance based on learning targets

targets also creates less demand on the coach to serve as the resident expert regarding what the students should know and be able to do. The process becomes less personal, less focused on how the teacher did, and more about closing the gap between what students can do and what they need to be able to do.

Get Close to the Students as the Learning Happens

Noticing and naming demands that we are close to the action when learning is taking place. When coaches stand back or stay out of the way, the default conversation becomes about student engagement or behavior, rather than on what the students are doing as learners. There is no question that it is important to discuss student engagement and behavior when co-planning lessons with teachers, but we don't want to be limited to these areas. *Noticing and naming* is really about formative assessment, and formative assessment is about zeroing in on how our students are performing. That means we pull up a chair to talk with kids, read their writing, and dig in to learn what they are thinking.

QR Code 4.2
Noticing and Naming During a Third-Grade Reading Lesson

http://qrs.ly/5j59nuv

There are lots of ways to formatively assess. One of the most powerful is conferring. In their text *Rigorous Reading*, Nancy Frey and Douglas Fisher (2013) write, "Conferring provides the teacher with an excellent assessment opportunity. These conferences allow the teacher to gauge the progress of each student, clarify information, and provide feedback for next steps. In addition, teachers keep records of these conferences for later reflection about individual student progress" (p. 117).

At times, the coach and teacher may choose to fan out and confer with different students and then share their notes during a planning conversation. Or, another option is for the coach and teacher to co-confer with students and discuss what they are learning as the students are engaged in authentic learning. While on the surface this may seem less efficient, we find it to be quite the opposite. Collectively making meaning of student learning as it happens decreases the necessity of finding the time to discuss it later with the teacher and in turn saves time. Furthermore, *noticing and naming* in the moment can lead to immediate feedback for the student and new thinking for how the teacher will design future instruction. But conferring isn't our only way to *notice and name.* We can also get close to students during small group instruction, independent work, and group work. Any opportunity when students are engaged as learners is a great time to *notice and name.*

Clearly Articulate What the Students Did Well and Where They Can Grow ... After Asking What the Teacher Thinks

Coaches often wonder how much information a coach should provide versus how much comes directly from the teacher. We have to be careful to avoid using *noticing and naming* as a blank check to talk *at* teachers about what we noticed during the lesson. Taking over the thinking in this way shuts downs the teachers' reflection and erodes the partnership that we work so hard to build.

While we know that leaving the interpretation and thinking up to the teacher is important, it is a very easy thing to forget to do. Diane recently made this mistake during a math lesson. The focus was on writing numbers in expanded form, and the teacher had developed an exit slip to formatively assess the students (see Figure 4.2).

During the lesson, the teacher reviewed the concept of expanded notation. Then the students worked through a few examples on whiteboards.

Figure 4.2 Formative Assessment of Expanded Form

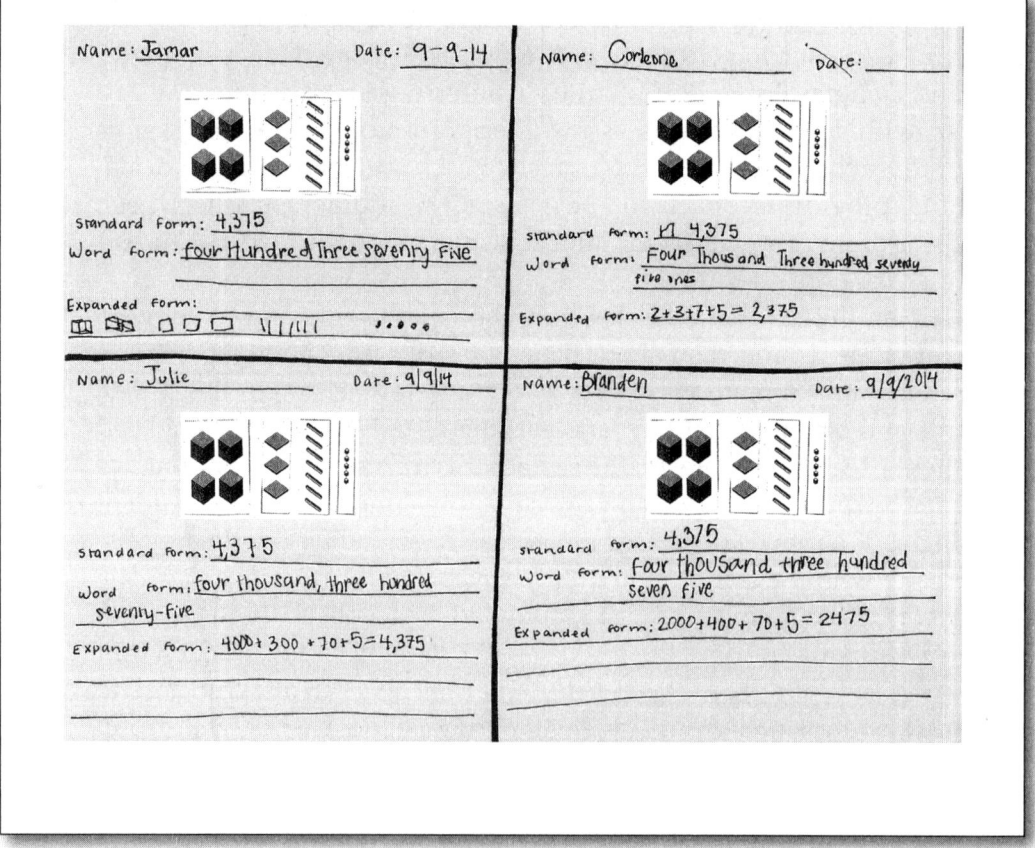

As the students got started on the exit slip, Diane and the teacher conferred with students to see how they approached the problem. It didn't take long for a few common misconceptions to jump out at Diane. She noticed that many of the students were able to look at the diagram and represent it in standard form. She noticed that some of the students were able to write the number correctly in word form, while others weren't. And she noticed that almost all of the students were unsure about how to write in expanded form. This was interesting because expanded form had been the focus of the lesson. These observations led her to so many thoughts and questions. She wondered, "What if the students had more chances to practice expanded form? How else could it have been modeled? Do they understand why each way of representing numbers is important? Is it the size of the number that is tricky for them?"

This is where we have to be careful as coaches. We get so excited by seeing the students engage as learners, that we sometimes put our own thinking first, rather than asking the teacher what she thinks. And as they debriefed the lesson, Diane did just that. She sat down with the teacher and said, "Did you notice how many students were confused by writing the number in expanded form?" Then she went on to share all of the things that she could do about it. As a result, Diane unintentionally shut down a pathway for the teacher to learn and make meaning. If she had begun the conversation with "What did you notice your students doing well?" and "What are some possible areas where we can take them further?," Diane likely would have learned far more from the teacher, gone further to build their partnership, and increased the teacher's reflection. Instead, she made the mistake of doing the thinking for the teacher, which is never a good idea.

Plan for Noticing and Naming

Some of our most important instructional decision making is determining how we will make the students' learning visible during the lesson. Thinking through what the students will learn, how their conversations will be structured, how their thinking will be captured in written form, and what we hope to hear them saying is all part of planning for *noticing and naming.*

Imagine this example: An eighth-grade teacher and literacy coach are planning a lesson with the learning target "I can notice how an author makes an argument that is engaging to the reader." Their plan is to make the students' learning visible by asking them to read and annotate a mentor text about banning sugary drinks. While reading the text, the students will work in groups of three to discuss what they noticed about how the author crafted the argument. While these discussions take place, the teacher and coach sit with the small groups to listen in and note what they are hearing. At certain points in the conversation, they may clarify vocabulary or redirect students, but mostly they will listen. Later, the students will share their thinking with the whole class, providing another opportunity to *notice and name*. Finally, the students will work on their own writing projects. In their writer's notebooks, they will jot down their own ideas for how they will craft an argument when they write their piece. At this stage, the coach and teacher co-confer with a few students who may need a bit of extra support. Through careful planning, a single lesson can provide five opportunities for *noticing and naming* (see Figure 4.3).

The only time we come up empty when using the strategy of *noticing and naming* is when students aren't given the opportunity to engage as *learners* . . . but instead are treated as *listeners*. Diane recently had this experience in a high school classroom that she visited. The teacher and coach were setting up a new tech tool, and they walked the students through every step of the process without giving them much opportunity to uncover the purpose for the tool, how they might envision using it, or even what they thought about it. As she entered the classroom, Diane was prepared with a grid for collecting student evidence, much like you saw in Figure 3.3. But as she left the classroom, the grid remained empty; a sure sign that the students spent the full class period listening to the teacher. This only reinforces the importance of co-planning. Before a lesson even begins, it is important for the coach and teacher to determine what the students will do in order to demonstrate their understandings. Without this, there will be no formative assessment. And without any formative assessment, there will be no *noticing and naming*.

Figure 4.3 Examples of Noticing and Naming

Task	Type of Evidence
Student annotations of the text	Written demonstration of the students' thinking
Student discussions of the text	Oral demonstration through small groups
Whole class share session	Oral demonstration through discussion
Use of writer's notebooks	Written demonstration at the independent level
Conferences with students	Oral and written demonstration through discussion

Plan for What Comes After Noticing and Naming

The coaching move *noticing and naming* not only helps the teacher and coach make instructional decisions in the moment, but it can also lead them right into planning the next lesson. The following example is from a coach and teacher who are working on writing summaries with a class of fifth graders. As the students worked, the coach and teacher rotated around the classroom and conferred with students. Then they quickly checked in at the end of the lesson to share what they noticed. Here's what they said:

Coach: I'm seeing a lot of students who are writing long summaries that include a series of events rather than the main idea. Did you see the same thing?

Teacher: Yes, I noted a few students who are doing that as well. I also noticed that a few students are giving a general main idea, but they aren't backing it up with examples. That's what we've been working on, so I'm surprised to see this happening.

Coach: So that's two patterns. One is listing events. Another is giving more of a generic main idea. Let's talk more about this when we meet to plan on Friday. Oh, and can you bring their summaries with you? We can look at those as well.

Teacher: Yes, no problem.

Noticing and naming gave the teacher and coach just what they needed to dive into planning for the next week. While the coach worked in the classroom two to three days a week, they always sat down to plan on Fridays. During this time, they followed a predictable pattern. First, they discussed what the students did as learners. Then, they planned what to do about it. This simple structure allowed them to dive into the student evidence and make decisions based upon it.

LESSONS FROM THE FIELD

Norma is a seventh-grade math teacher in a school district north of Denver. Leanna has been coaching Norma and her team for the better part of the school year. An emphasis has been on using student-friendly learning targets and formatively assessing on a continual basis. As they work together with Norma's class, they have the opportunity to think

(Continued)

(Continued)

about how this looks during classroom instruction and in planning for next steps after the lesson.

Leanna asks, "What are you thinking about for today's lesson?" Norma jumps in, "After we talk through the learning target and introduce the problem, I was planning to work with a small group. It would be great if you would listen in as the other table groups get started." Leanna nods. "Great. Is there anything you'd like me to look for when I'm sitting with the table groups?" Norma says, "Ideally, you can see if the problems they are writing are what we hope to see. I want to reteach any areas that are confusing them." Leanna agrees, and they grab their things and head to Norma's classroom.

For the last few weeks, Norma and her students have been working on two math standards: (1) *Use properties of operations to generate equivalent expressions*, and (2) *solve real-life and mathematical problems using numerical and algebraic expressions and equations*. After building their understanding of expressions, equations, and order of operations, Norma would like her students to go from a real-life situation to a mathematical expression (decontextualize) and from an expression to a real-life situation (contextualize). At this point in the coaching cycle, Norma and Leanna are working on two straightforward learning targets (see Figure 4.4):

Figure 4.4 Learning Targets

1. I can use the order of operations to create and solve expressions that represent real-life situations.
2. I can use a mathematical expression to create a real-life situation.

For today's lesson, Norma will be introducing the second learning target, giving the students an expression, $(5 \times \$1.25 + 3 \times \$.75 + \$2.50)24$, and asking them to create a real-life story that represents the problem. As the students get to work, Leanna circulates and listens in as the groups tackle the problem. Because some of the numbers in the expression are monetary, a few groups frame their story around buying certain amounts of different items. Leanna notes this evidence of understanding. As she moves to another group, she sees that they have no words written down, just numbers. She listens in as Hailey talks through her attempt to solve the expression. Ivan sits next to Hailey and says, "For the second part I got 3 × .75 = 2.25." This makes Leanna wonder because the students had been learning that an expression is a mathematical phrase that may contain numbers, variables, and operations. An equation is a math sentence that says that two things are equal. 5 + 3 is an expression. 5 + 3 = 8 is an equation. Leanna jots down, "Do the students understand the difference between expressions and equations?"

As Norma finishes up with her small group, Leanna gives her a quick update on what she's *noticing* around the room. They agree that they don't want Hailey's group to spend the whole work time going down the wrong path, so they decide to intervene with some focused instruction, or *naming*, what they feel the students need to keep them moving toward the learning target.

They head to Hailey's table, and Norma begins by asking them to tell her what they're working on. Jana jumps right in and says, "We're trying to solve the problem because we don't think you can come up with a real world story if you don't know the answer." The rest of the group nods in agreement. Leanna draws their attention back to the learning target posted at the front of the room. "Your target for today is 'I can use a mathematical expression to create a real-life situation.' Does it say anything about finding the answer?" They acknowledge that it does not. Then she decides to pose this question, "If I gave you the expression 7 – 4, could you make up a story to go with it?" Trevor nods. "Yeah, you could say I have 7 cookies and my brother ate 4." "Okay," Leanna confirms. "Trevor has shown us that you can create a story without needing to know the answer, right?" But Hailey persists, "That's an easy problem. You can't do it with something harder." Norma offers a multistep problem to continue to challenge their thinking. The students keep working for several more minutes. Then Norma wraps up the lesson by asking a few groups to share what they've come up with. The bell rings, and the students are dismissed.

Later, when Norma and Leanna meet to plan, they begin by talking through how the lesson went. Norma shares what she thought about the small group they had worked with. She felt they were getting there, but she realized how much more support they will need to meet the learning targets. Then they review the student work that was collected during the class period. First, they examine the anecdotal notes that they gathered. Then they match their notes up with the work that was turned in. This provides them with two corresponding pieces of evidence to reflect and plan from.

(Continued)

> (Continued)
>
> After this general review of the student work, Norma and Leanna divide the students into three groups: those who understood all aspects of the problem and were able to create a coherent story problem that represented the expression, those who got a good start to the problem and could represent what was inside the parenthesis but didn't know what to do with the number that was outside, and finally those who still needed support with order of operations and how it can be represented in a real-life context.
>
> Having a clear sense of where the students are in relation to the learning targets helps them jump right in to planning instruction for the three groups. They decide that their first step will be to provide the small group with follow-up instruction on the order of operations. Norma has lots of ideas for how she will reteach this. Then they discuss pairing up the rest of the students into heterogeneous partnerships so the students will be able support one another through more practice with a similar problem. This will provide an authentic opportunity to extend the learning of both groups, either through the role of teacher or learner. They spend a few more minutes finalizing their plan for instruction—a plan that is based on what they *noticed* and *named* during the lesson.

TOOLS AND TECHNIQUES

Troubleshooting Conversations About Noticing and Naming

Noticing and naming may feel awkward at first. The teacher may worry that it will bother the students. And the coach may worry about interjecting too much during a lesson. The coach's best bet is to discuss why *noticing and naming* is a good idea and what it will look like. Here's some language you may use to set up an environment when *noticing and naming* can occur (see Figure 4.5).

Figure 4.5 Language for *Noticing and Naming*

If I hear . . .	Then I can use the following language . . .
I'm worried that it may be distracting to my students if you interject during the lesson.	We will be discrete about how and when we share. When we plan, you can let me know what feels best. And it's actually good for students to know where they are in relation to the learning targets.

If I hear . . .	Then I can use the following language . . .
Will it make the students feel bad?	We will make sure that we focus on the positive as well as what would stretch the students further. You can expect something like this, "Miguel is doing a great job using evidence in his summary. It looks like he is still working on his sequencing."
Will this take any more work?	I don't think so. We already have our weekly planning meeting set up so we are in good shape. And *noticing and naming* during the lesson just means that we are looking for the same things and taking notes that we can look at later.

Collecting Conference Notes

When we are less familiar with the content that we are coaching, such as when we are coaching in a variety of subjects in middle and high schools, co-teaching can feel a bit unnerving. However, if the learning targets are clear, then we should be able to collect student evidence that will lead to informed instructional decision making, no matter what the subject matter.

Figure 4.6 provides an example of how to collect conference notes to serve as student evidence. Including each student in the grid reminds the teacher and coach to collect student evidence for each and every student.

Figure 4.6 Conference Notes

Learning Targets:

- I can summarize what I read.
- I can identify the theme of a fictional text.
- I can infer how the theme affects the characters in the story.

Abby	*Karma*
Unsure about the theme. Can summarize the story.	Able to name a theme for the text. Mentioned characters while discussing the theme.

(Continued)

Figure 4.6 (Continued)

Becky	Jonathan
Able to name a theme for the text. Inferred as well.	Connected with the characters' feelings. Not sure about theme.
Daniel	Paige
Infers to think toward theme. Uses the language, "I'm thinking that . . . "	Unsure of the theme. She shares some details from the text rather than providing a summary.

It also assures teachers that as coaches we are there to learn from their students, rather than to focus if they are (or aren't) doing a good job.

Collecting Other Anecdotal Evidence

Sometimes we like to remind ourselves to collect data that is multifaceted. We can learn so much by listening to students as they discuss their thinking or by looking over their shoulders to see what they are writing. And if we are working on a goal that centers on student engagement, it might be helpful to collect student evidence around what the students are actually doing across the class period. Figure 4.7 reminds us that data is manifested in so many different ways.

Figure 4.7 Student Evidence—Doing, Saying, and Writing

Learning Targets:

I observed students doing:

I heard students saying:

I saw students writing:

A FINAL THOUGHT

We can learn a lot from coaches like the basketball coach that helped his team win the state championship. We accomplish this by keeping a close watch on student learning as it happens and then naming how the current demonstration of learning stacks up against what we hope to see as the students progress toward mastery of the standards. As learners, we sometimes have a difficult time knowing what to do next. When we have someone there, watching over our shoulder, talking with us, and looking at our work, then we are more likely to feel as if we are on track.

As coaches, we find ourselves *noticing and naming* every time we are in classrooms. We watch the students, listen to their thinking, and determine what might take them further. It is one of the most powerful coaching moves because it can be done on a continual basis. If coaches wonder what they should do while they are in classrooms working side by side with teachers, the first suggestion would always be to *notice and name* because it provides them with a vision for how to partner with teachers in a way that is entirely focused on what the students are doing well and where they have potential to grow as learners. As a result, we walk away from a lesson with rich data, or student evidence, that informs the instruction that we will deliver—in the next moment or the next day.

[Handwritten notes at top: Shared partnership / Be precise, roles are clear / Words you can say to help teacher — shared ownership / Elbow partner]

5 Micro Modeling

[Handwritten: Gradual Release / scaffo / Coteaching / I Do / We Do / You Do]

As the teachers gathered in the school library for the last staff meeting of the year, most were thinking about packing up their classrooms and getting started with their summer plans. But the principal wanted to share some exciting news before she sent them on their way. Thanks to a new district initiative, a staff developer from Denver would be coming to work with the teachers on reading comprehension over the upcoming school year. It was 1998, and teaching students to better comprehend texts was making a significant impact on how we approached teaching reading. Gone were the dittos, thankfully replaced by rich conversation about interesting text. And since Prairie View Elementary didn't have funding for a school-based coach, the principal wasn't about to turn down this offer. As a fifth-grade teacher, David was also thrilled to hear the news. He had been working on the very same thing with his students and welcomed the idea of coaching. He even volunteered his classroom to host the observations that would be part of the project.

Diane also looked forward to working with the teachers at Prairie View. She had recently left her own fifth-grade classroom and was new to coaching. In the past, she had benefited from observing lessons, so she suggested that they design a coaching plan that would begin with her modeling a few lessons in different teachers' classrooms. Both she and the principal felt that modeling would be a good way to paint a picture of what it looked like to teach reading comprehension.

David's fifth graders craned their necks as the teachers filed in for the first model lesson. They weren't used to seeing other teachers in their room, and as Diane settled in on the rocking chair at the front of the room, Sammy couldn't resist raising her hand and saying, "So, who are you anyway?" Diane smiled and explained that she was a literacy coach who was working with the teachers at Prairie View. That's why they would have observers during reading time. Then she added, "Today we are going to

[Handwritten at bottom: ★ Set expectations]

think about what good readers do while they are reading. I will introduce a few strategies that you can use to better understand what you read."

As the teachers observed, Diane proceeded to model how readers stop and think across a text. The students raised their hands enthusiastically and loved the book that Diane had chosen. She felt great and couldn't wait to debrief with the team of teachers to talk over what they noticed during the lesson.

While they walked down the hallway to the library, David mentioned in an almost apologetic tone, "That was a great lesson. But I thought I'd let you know that I taught the same lesson a few days ago." Diane was horrified. She couldn't believe that she had modeled an entire lesson that had already been taught. She was supposed to be supporting teacher development, not wasting people's time. Then David added reassuringly, "But I liked seeing how you approached it. And my kids loved it." That's when Diane thought, "No more dog-and-pony shows. There must be a better way."

A lot has changed since then. Thankfully, now that we coach in cycles with a clear goal that leads to thoughtful plans for instruction, we no longer just swoop in to coach out of context. And our partnership approach to coaching means that our days of only modeling lessons have become a thing of the past, too.

THE MOVE—*MICRO MODELING*

Micro modeling is a strategy where a coach models a small portion of the instructional block rather than the whole thing. It serves the important role of providing visual examples for teachers while also allowing the coach and teacher to share ownership over what is taught, something that is often missing when a coach is up in front of the room and teaching her heart out for an entire lesson (like Diane did in David's room).

As coaches, we love to teach. In fact, many of us miss having our own classroom and the connection that it provides with students. In some ways, this longing to teach may create the conditions that lead to too much modeling. When one person is sitting passively while the other does all of the teaching, we aren't doing much to create a partnership. And if coaching is about co-constructing learning with teachers, then it's worth thinking about how we use the strategy of modeling. We aren't saying that modeling isn't an important tool for coaching. We just think modeling can be done with more precision and purpose.

Micro modeling is an important tool to use not only during a lesson but also throughout a coaching cycle. It allows the coach and teacher to support each other to deliver instruction that meets the needs of students.

It is a flexible and dynamic process that includes the voice of the teacher and coach. There are times when it makes sense to demonstrate a particular instructional practice. For example, a coach may model how to provide feedback to students, may teach a portion of a lesson, or may lead a small group while a teacher observes. Providing a visual of what good instruction looks like is an essential component of how coaches work in classrooms. It's just not all that we do.

WHY *MICRO MODELING* IS IMPORTANT

Over the years, our thinking has changed when it comes to how the Gradual Release of Responsibility model applies to adult learners (Pearson and Gallagher, 1983). In *Student-Centered Coaching,* Diane (Sweeney, 2011) shared how Angie organized her coaching using this framework. "First, they planned a few days' worth of mini-lessons that Angie modeled while Paula observed and took notes. At the end of each week, they reflected on the student work and instruction to decide what to do next. The second stage came a few weeks into the cycle with Paula planning and co-teaching alongside Angie. With time, they shifted to Paula doing most of the teaching on her own, just as Angie had promised" (p. 93).

As we have become more student-centered in our coaching, we now realize that the idea of adult learners progressing neatly through the stages of "I do, we do, you do" seems a bit too tidy in the real world of coaching. Whereas we know how important the gradual release of responsibility is when working with kids and still advocate for planning using an "I do, we do, you do" structure, we just don't think it applies to adult learners. We are spending more time than ever in the "we do" stage, because this is where partnerships are built. This approach allows us to create a shared effort, no matter how many years of experience a teacher might have.

We limit our time in the "I do" stage because we avoid operating under the assumption that teachers have nothing to bring to the conversation unless we show them how to do it. We would never want to imply that the coach is the expert, and the teacher isn't. Too much time in the "I do" stage can erode the partnerships that we are trying to create. We also spend less time in the "you do" stage because we have found that observing teachers can feel evaluative. We make exceptions if teachers request to be observed in order to receive feedback on a specific instructional practice. Of course we will respond to these types of requests. But we really do believe that our power lies in the "we do" stage, and that's where we try to spend most of our time when we are in classrooms.

WHAT *MICRO MODELING* LOOKS LIKE

Micro modeling is one of the many ways we coach while in the classroom. We have both benefited from seeing great models of instruction, and the last thing we'd want to suggest is that modeling is not an effective coaching practice. Rather, our shift has been to model with intention and in a way that builds on, rather than dismantles, our partnerships with teachers. Here's what *micro modeling* looks like.

**QR Code 5.1
Micro Modeling During a Third-Grade Reading Lesson**

http://qrs.ly/vz59nux

Micro Model During Whole Group, Small Group, or One-On-One Instruction

The power of *micro modeling* isn't limited to whole group lessons. It can be equally as effective during small group and one-on-one instruction. In the essay *Content Coaching*, Lucy West (2008) writes, "In this coaching practice, we do not 'divide and conquer,' we 'stick together.' What I mean by this is a coach rarely works with one group of students while the teacher works with another. Instead, they travel from student to student or group to group as a team" (p. 138). What West is describing creates the perfect conditions for *micro modeling* to occur because modeling even a single conversation presents invaluable opportunities for teachers to construct meaning about teaching and learning. When a coach and teacher sit together during conferences, they are in a better position to grow in their practice. The coach may *micro model* the first conference, and then they can co-confer from there. The key is that this decision is shared, and modeling is presented as one of many options for how the coach and teacher may work together with students.

Micro modeling during small groups is also an effective strategy to build teacher capacity. Working side by side during small groups presents the opportunity for a coach to *micro model* what makes the most sense in the moment. While it may be tempting to fan out and cover more territory during conferences or small groups, we suggest using this time to learn and grow together.

Support Implementation . . . and Stay Student-Centered

Modeling is often a go-to strategy when a district is implementing a new program or curriculum. A district that is switching from basal reading instruction to reader's workshop may decide that teachers would benefit from seeing what it looks like. This makes a lot of sense. Modeling can be an effective strategy to get started with implementation. But sooner or later, teachers need help implementing it themselves. This is where *micro modeling* can be an effective coaching move.

Let's take the example of Heather, who is featured later in this chapter. As a brand-new coach in a district that recently adopted a rigorous math program, Heather is responsible for helping teachers understand the math content and program materials, while keeping the focus on what the students are learning. Effectively, Heather coaches the implementation of a math program while also being student-centered.

Micro modeling is one of the moves that Heather uses while coaching in the classroom. As she and teachers work through their math lessons, they continually question, "How are the students doing, and what should we do next?" In a single lesson, they hand the instructional baton back and forth. Each handoff involves transitions where Heather may *micro model* or where the teacher may take the lead. It is a dynamic process that merges her role as a student-centered coach and program implementer.

Plan With (Not for) the Teacher

It is difficult to *micro model* if a coach and teacher aren't on the same page regarding a lesson. And since coaching in the classroom is based on partnerships with teachers, it is best to avoid planning lessons for them. Some coaches put in countless hours planning gorgeous lessons that they will turn around and model for teachers. In *The Literacy Coach's Game Plan*, Sadder and Nidus (2009) write, "The role of the coach is not to show an airbrushed version of a lesson but rather to roll up her sleeves and demonstrate the gritty aspects of teaching a lesson, including planning, teaching, preparing, and reflecting. So, too, the teacher's role moves from being an adoring or critical audience member to an active participant in the demonstration" (p. 106).

We'd argue that when a coach plans lessons without the teacher, precious learning is lost. Questions like "How will the learning target be introduced? What will the students do to engage with new learning? What will be modeled? How will student dialogue be supported? What kinds of problems or tasks will make the students' learning visible?" are important to work through together. When we plan together, the decisions (and ownership) are shared. And when decisions are shared, it is easier for the coach and teacher to determine if *micro modeling* is the right strategy.

If a coach makes instructional decisions in isolation, there is also a decreased likelihood that teachers will follow through when the coach is gone. The reason for this is simple; we have a hard time following through on something that we didn't have a hand in creating. When coaches ask, "Why aren't teachers owning it? I feel like when I leave, they'll stop doing whatever we've been working on," our answer usually comes back to the matter of shared ownership. If we co-plan, then we are more likely to see teachers following through because the learning was co-constructed from the beginning.

Define Who Will Do What

Diane and Leanna both have teenagers at home, and one of their favorite words is *"Awkward!"* While our kids are usually talking about the embarrassing things we do as middle-aged parents, it can also apply to coaching in someone else's classroom.

We find that the easiest way to handle this uncertainty is to face it head on. Before a lesson even begins, it can be helpful to ask the teacher, "What would you like to do?" and "What would you like me to do?" The goal is to establish a shared effort throughout the lesson, no matter what level of skill the teacher may have. Even the newest teachers have something to bring to the table when we are working alongside them in their classrooms. If things feel *"Awkward,"* then it might make sense to establish clarity regarding how the next lesson will be shared.

We accomplish this by segmenting lessons so that we can plan logical transitions throughout. In this way, the coach and teacher can determine who will take on each section. *Micro modeling* can then fit within the part of the lesson that makes the most sense based what the teacher is working on. The following coaching log is designed for this purpose (see Figure 5.1).

QR Code 5.2
Micro Modeling During a Middle School Math Lesson

http://qrs.ly/6859nuy

Stay Focused on What the Teacher Is Working On

While we frame coaching cycles around a goal for student learning, teachers may also identify instructional goals that they would like to work on. A good rule of thumb for *micro modeling* is to stay focused on the instructional practice that was identified by the teacher. In today's era of teacher evaluation, there is no shortage of instructional goals floating around in teachers' heads. The common refrain of "I'm supposed to be . . . " is always hanging in the air and can be an easy place for coaches to decide where to suggest *micro modeling* as a support for teacher learning. The key is that we model based on areas that have been named by the teacher, not by us. Breaking this rule leads to a shift from coaching that is a partnership to one that is about fixing teachers.

Figure 5.1 Planner for Sharing Lessons

Eighth-Grade Reading With James (the teacher) and Lisa (the coach)

What's Happening	What It Will Look Like	Who Will Take the Lead? What Will the Other "Teacher" Do?
Reflect on the Learning Target	Students will reflect on the learning target with a partner. *Learning Target: I can analyze how the form or structure of a text contributes to its meaning and style.*	Lisa *micro models* this part of the lesson. James has set this as a goal for his teaching and would like Lisa to demonstrate what it looks like to have students self-assess against a learning target. As Lisa *micro models,* she will *think aloud* so that James gets a sense of what she is thinking throughout this portion of the lesson.
Mini Lesson	In the lesson, James will remind the students of the following elements of fiction: plot, character, setting, and conflict. This will be review. Then, he will use examples of familiar literature to illustrate how fiction writers create structure around these elements. James will think aloud using a book that he is currently reading where each chapter is written in the voice of a different character. He will explain how this lends itself to a character-based plot structure. Lastly, he will think aloud about how the structure supports the overall meaning of the book.	James teaches the mini lesson. He requests that Lisa clarify and add on if she notices any confusion. She may also redirect any students who aren't engaged.
Discussion Groups	Students work in small groups to discuss the texts they are reading. Their prompt is, *Which is the most dominant feature of your book: plot, character, setting, or conflict? How does this contribute to the overall meaning of the book?*	Lisa and James work with small groups. Their plan is to stick together so they can hear the same conversations. This way they will be able to take what they hear into account when they co-plan.
Reflect	After the small groups, the students reflect on the learning target one more time. This is done on an index card and is turned in at the end of the class period.	Lisa and James collect student evidence by listening to what the students say and how they explain their thinking. They also review the index cards during their co-planning session.

Imagine a teacher who would like to focus on students selecting "just right" books. But while the coach is in the classroom, she notices that the reading lessons are stretching on, and the students are losing focus and becoming disengaged. A coach's first instinct is to suggest modeling a more focused lesson and then hoping that the teacher will realize that she should have been doing this all along. This shortcut often leads nowhere, however, except to frustration and loss of trust among teachers.

Take a Strengths-Based Approach

If we hope to create coaching relationships that are built on trust and respect, then we are best served by believing in teachers. Believing that they are competent, that they care about their students, and that they are able to learn and grow is an essential component of creating relationships where teachers will feel comfortable taking the risks that learning demands. With almost thirty years of coaching experience between the two of us, we know that this can be challenging. We have been in situations when we were worried about kids, or when we felt uneasy about what we were seeing in terms of instruction. In these situations, it is tempting to slip into a mentality of "Move over, I'll take it from here." This approach can then lead to more modeling than we intended to do. We must continually remind ourselves that what we are asking teachers to do is complex and challenging, so honoring this is essential if we are going to build trusting relationships where coaching will thrive.

LESSONS FROM THE FIELD

Earlier in this chapter, we introduced Heather, an elementary math coach. Part of the reason Heather was hired to be a coach was because of her incredible content knowledge in mathematics. In fact, on her summers off, Heather works as a staff developer for the company who created the math curriculum that is used in her district. She is a true expert, which is often tricky territory for a school-based coach. It is territory that might be ripe for an approach that includes model, model, and model some more. But rather than parachuting into classrooms and teaching fantastic lessons, Heather views her role as being about building teacher ownership and capacity. She knows that this won't happen if she does all of the thinking for teachers.

It was early in the school year when Diane visited Heather's school in O'Fallon, Missouri. The district was in the beginning stages of implementing coaching, and when they sat down together, Heather asked a familiar question "I want to know if I'm doing this right. Does it look like coaching?" As a former classroom teacher, Heather knew how to approach her work, but coaching felt less defined, and she wanted feedback.

Diane spent the morning shadowing Heather as she worked with Robyn, a fourth-grade teacher. Robyn was new to the profession and had an energetic class of students. Heather and Robyn had planned the lesson on the day prior and knew what they wanted to accomplish (see Figure 5.2).

First and foremost, they were hoping to see if the students were using the methods they had been teaching for composing and decomposing numbers. They began the lesson with a two-digit multiplication problem that would serve as a formative assessment. Robyn wrote the problem on the board and prompted the students to find a solution using one of the methods that they had learned over the past few days. Heather passed out half sheets of paper and reminded the students to show their work. As the students finished up, Heather and Robyn took the student work to the back counter and quickly sorted it into three piles (got it, getting there, needs more support). Then they spent a few minutes talking through what they noticed. Heather asked, "Based on what you see here, do you feel like we are ready to move on to three digit numbers, or do you think we should stick with two-digit problems for a while longer?" Robyn said, "I think they should stick with two digit numbers." Heather nodded and probed, "What are you noticing that makes you feel that way?" Robyn responded, "I see that some of the students have the idea of what they're doing, but they aren't finishing out the part where they find the sums." "Ok," said Heather, "so how about if we throw out another two-digit problem and then we can scaffold into some three-digit problems after that?" Robyn agreed, "Ok, that sounds good to me."

In just a few minutes, Heather and Robyn had formatively assessed, analyzed the student work, and adjusted their instruction. Their next step would be for Heather to *micro model* during the guided practice stage of instruction. In the planning session, they had decided that the students would solve a series of problems on whiteboards so that they could continue to formatively assess. At one moment when the students were hard at work, Heather said, "Let's take a walk" and

(Continued)

(Continued)

Figure 5.2 Fourth Grade Mathematics Lesson With Heather and Robyn

What's Happening?	What Will It Look Like?	Who Will Take the Lead? What Will the Other "Teacher" Do?
Formative Assessment	Students will solve the following problem to assess the strategies they are using when they encounter two-digit multiplication. The problem is 57 × 33. The students will solve the problem on half sheets so that the coach and teacher can quickly sort them before the reteach.	Robyn will get the students started with the problem. Then they will collect and sort the student evidence.
Guided Practice	Students solve more problems that are determined based on how they did with the formative assessment. This time they will work on whiteboards. Showing how they solved the problem will be emphasized. An anchor chart will be used to capture the different methods that the students are using.	Heather will *micro model* how she assesses problem-solving strategies. Robyn and Heather will monitor student learning and check in with each other to determine how to scaffold students' learning.
Share	Students share how they went about solving the problems. As they share, they will be asked if this is the most efficient strategy and if they got the correct answer.	Heather and Robyn will teach this in tandem.

led Robyn from table to table so they could look for the methods students were using to solve the problems. This helped Robyn understand some of the students' errors and misconceptions and went a long way in building her capacity as a teacher of mathematics. With this new insight, Robyn led the students through a few more problems while Heather looked on. Her confidence was noticeably building, and Heather was right there to make sure she was successful.

As Diane observed, she wondered how in the world Heather could be wondering if she was an effective coach. When they sat down after the lesson, their first matter of business was to celebrate the students' learning. A math curriculum specialist had also observed the lesson and asked how long they had been working on composing and decomposing numbers. When she learned that this was the first week, she was speechless. This group of fourth graders was moving further and faster than she had ever seen, and they had a first year teacher at the helm. There was no question that Heather's partnership in the classroom was impacting student learning.

TOOLS AND TECHNIQUES

Troubleshooting Conversations About Modeling

Many teachers expect coaching to consist mostly of modeling. Others may resist coaching because they aren't interested in modeling. Moving past these existing perceptions may take some time and intentional conversations about the role of a coach and the practices that a coach may use while in the classroom. Figure 5.3 provides an if/then chart to help coaches troubleshoot conversations about modeling.

Figure 5.3 Language for Micro Modeling

If I hear . . .	Then I can use the following language . . .
Can you model another lesson? You are such a great math teacher, and I don't feel like I know what I'm doing.	I'd be more than happy to *micro model* a certain part of the lesson. Which part would you feel would be most beneficial to have modeled?
[A principal says] I'd like you to show our teachers what it looks like. It is a new program and they need help getting started.	We can provide a few opportunities for teachers to observe what it looks like. But then I'd like to start helping them implement on their own. This will involve some targeted *micro modeling* but probably not a whole lesson because I'd like to create ownership to build their capacity.
I'm not really interested in coaching. I've observed plenty of lessons and I know what I'm doing.	I understand. I don't do a lot of modeling, but when I do, it is something specific that you ask for. Otherwise, we work as partners while in your classroom.

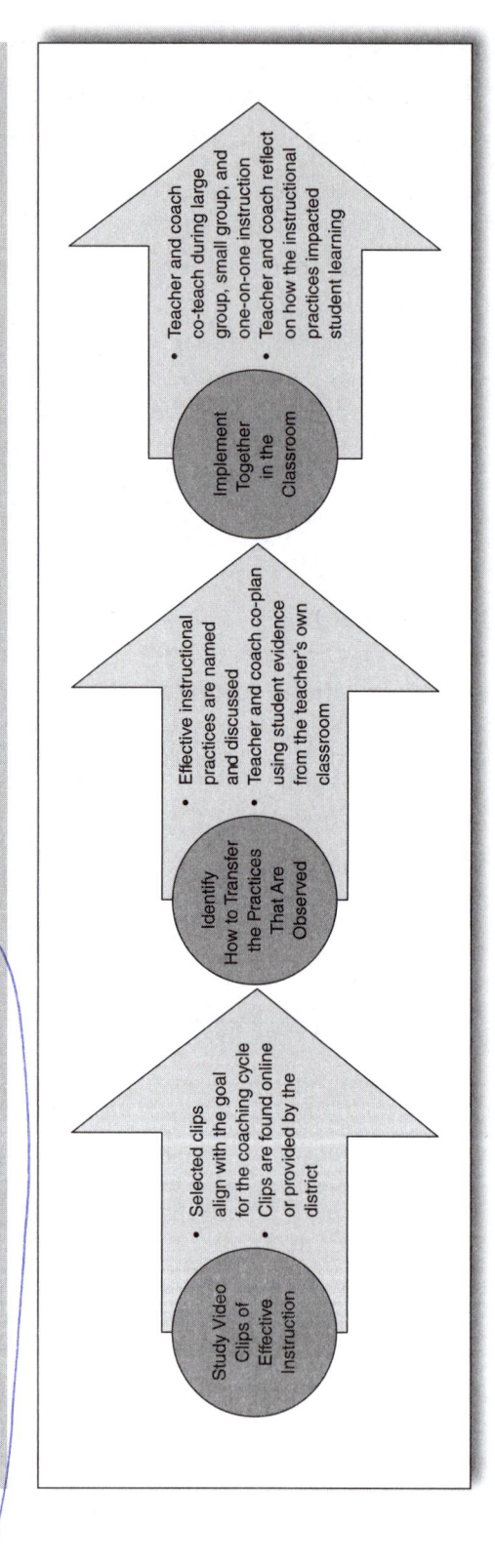

Figure 5.4 Micro Modeling Using Video

Video and Micro Modeling

Video is an effective tool for *micro modeling*. Many districts are creating libraries of lessons that align with their expectations for the delivery of instruction. For example, Liberty School District in Missouri is currently implementing readers' and writers' workshop across grades K–12. Their district website includes short video clips of what it looks like to teach using the workshop model. While teachers may choose to use these resources on their own, an even more powerful practice is to embed these resources right into a coaching cycle. In this way, the coach can scaffold the teachers' thinking in a way that transfers what they see in the video clip to their own work with students.

Engaging in the use of videos also alleviates the pressure of the coach as expert. Rather than modeling the teaching yourself, it can be beneficial to study others as they teach. There are many opportunities throughout a coaching cycle to dip into video clips in this way. For example, a teacher may be interested in learning strategies for conferring with students. The coach may select a few clips of effective conferences to analyze and then practice with students. This simple protocol goes a long way in building the instructional practices within a student-centered coaching cycle. Figure 5.4 provides a vision for what it looks like to *micro model* using video.

Taking Micro Modeling to a Place of Reflection and Application

Micro modeling is most effective when it is coupled with dialogue and reflection. The questions in Figure 5.5 steer modeling toward teacher ownership and transfer to daily practice

Figure 5.5 Guiding Questions to Reflect on *Micro Modeling*

Questions to Ask Before *Micro Modeling*

1. What have you tried already? How did it go?
2. What impact has this had on your students?
3. Where are you feeling more or less comfortable? Why?

Questions to Ask After *Micro Modeling*

1. What did you notice about your students and their learning during the *micro modeling*?
2. What are some ways we may extend the student learning even further?
3. How did you see the students' thinking being scaffolded through dialogue and discussion?
4. How were the needs of different learners addressed (special education, English language learners, advanced learners)?

A FINAL THOUGHT

We understand that this chapter upsets the status quo in terms of recommended practices for instructional coaching. Most every coaching model advocates for modeling as the primary strategy for coaches to use when working in classrooms. Usually the Gradual Release of Responsibility is identified as the rationale for taking this approach. While we agree in theory, we find that modeling has gone too far in a lot of cases. If we overscaffold, handhold, or do the thinking for people, then we eliminate opportunities for them to learn and grow. This is true for both adults and our students. We hope that the idea of *micro modeling* creates a new vision for modeling without throwing out a commonly used practice that may make sense in certain situations.

We are finding that we aren't alone in this thinking. In fact, when we introduce the idea of *micro modeling* to coaches, it isn't uncommon to see a lot of nodding heads. After a recent presentation at a literacy conference, a coach approached Diane and said, "I'm so grateful to have come to your session. When I was hired, I never received any help with how to be a coach. I modeled lessons because I didn't know what else to do. Now I have a vision for coaching that will feel a lot more comfortable." We've all been there. Diane was mortified to realize her misstep when she took over David's class. Without intending to do so, she set up David to be a passive bystander who was expected to watch and learn.

Taking a more active approach with modeling also has the potential to dramatically impact the teacher and coach relationship. Most coaches aren't interested in being perceived as the expert, yet they so often depend on a coaching move that puts them in an expert role. We can take coaching to a more purposeful level with the simple step of being more intentional about how we use this important coaching move.

6 Thinking Aloud

In the late 1990s Diane and Leanna were working at the Denver-based Public Education and Business Coalition (PEBC) as staff developers—a precursor to what today are known as an instructional coaches. Much of their work was based upon the ground breaking book *Mosaic of Thought* (1997), written by the organization's founders Ellin Keene and Susan Zimmerman. The authors identified seven strategies that are part of a highly complex and metacognitive process that readers use to comprehend text. The premise was that to teach children how to understand what they read, this invisible process must be made visible. Unlike the decoding part of reading, which is visible in letters and words, it becomes necessary to get inside the brains of proficient readers to understand how they are using the thinking strategies to make sense of text. From this need was born the "think-aloud," or the notion of sharing your thinking so that others can learn from it.

When Leanna's daughter Lila recently received her learner's permit, she was anxious to learn to drive. As they began venturing out onto busy roads around town, the situation quickly became harried. Leanna found herself barking instructions at her daughter, which only increased Lila's sense of discomfort and uncertainty. "Do you see the cars slowing down ahead of you? You need to take your foot off the gas!" "Don't brake until you get all the way into the turn lane. Make sure the car in the left lane isn't going to pull out in front of you!" Things were not going well, and Leanna realized that something needed to change in her instruction.

Driving involves paying attention to myriad situations and making new decisions and adjustments all the time. As adults, this has become so second nature that we hardly notice it's happening, but for a new driver there is a lot to be thinking about at any given moment. Leanna connected this with the constant decision making faced by teachers and remembered the value of sharing her thinking with students. So she decided to give it a try with her daughter. The next few times she was driving with Lila, she spoke aloud about everything that was going through her head. "Right now, I'm looking at the car right in front of me, and I see brake lights, so I know I need to slow down. But up ahead I see that the light has just turned green so I'm going to get ready to accelerate again." "Even though I can make a right turn at the red light, I know that a lot of bikes ride by here, so I'm going to really watch out for that." By being metacognitive while driving, Leanna was not only telling Lila what to do, she was giving her insight into how and why she was making all of the various decisions needed to be a safe and effective driver.

Over the years, thinking aloud has become an important teaching practice across all grades and subject areas. In our work as coaches, we have also come to recognize it as a valuable move for student-centered coaching. It creates a dynamic interplay between teacher and coach where reflection and learning happen in the moment. When *thinking aloud,* we make the invisible process of teaching visible in our teacher-coach partnership.

THE MOVE—*THINKING ALOUD*

Thinking aloud is a coaching move that increases the metacognition and reflection that happen throughout a lesson. It most commonly occurs when a coach is co-teaching in a classroom. It sounds something like "We just gave the kids a really tough question to grapple with at their tables. I'm going to be listening in around the room to make sure their struggle is staying productive and that they're not getting too frustrated." Metacognitive thinking about instructional decisions is shared in the moment to maximize learning opportunities for students and to create openings for reflection and shared learning for the teacher and coach. While it fits quite naturally when co-teaching, it is also a useful strategy when planning and reflecting with teachers.

According to Imel (2002), "Metacognition refers to the ability of learners to be aware of and monitor their learning processes. Cognitive skills are those needed to perform a task, whereas metacognitive skills are necessary to understand how it was performed" (p. 3). When *thinking aloud,* both the teacher and coach share their thinking about their instructional decisions and how they are impacting student learning. In real time, they are saying, "Here is what I'm noticing, here's what I think we should do now, and this is why." Using this strategy provides the coach with more opportunities to address coachable moments as they happen, rather than waiting to talk about it later. *Thinking aloud* also allows the teacher and coach to gain insights into each other's metacognitive processes so that teaching can more easily be adjusted to meet the needs of students during any given lesson.

Coaching becomes more reflective

WHY *THINKING ALOUD* IS IMPORTANT

Like driving, teaching involves making countless on-the-spot decisions throughout a lesson. In a review of research studies on teacher decision making, Larry Cuban (2011) found that effective teachers have 200 to 300 mostly unpredictable interactions with students each hour, demanding that they "improvise—decide on the spot—as they deal with both the routine and unexpected."

In Chapter 2, we discussed how learning targets guide our plan for instruction, much like knowing where we want to go and how to get there in our car. But even with a general road map, we still need to adapt and respond to how our students are doing in class. At any given moment, some students may be getting it, and others may not. We ask, "Do we pull the whole class back together to discuss? Do we confer individually with those who are confused? Is their struggle likely to be beneficial to their learning? Should we wait and start the lesson tomorrow by having each student share with a partner?" So many decisions are being made all of the time, and yet how we make these decisions is an entirely invisible endeavor. When we share our thinking aloud, we make this process visible.

The coaching move *thinking aloud* is important because it enables us to accomplish two things. First, it allows us to share our knowledge about instructional strategies in the moment. Second, it gives us the opportunity to model being metacognitive, or thinking about our thinking. It is here where we are able to take the coaching conversation to a rich and reflective place because we are not only sharing the *what* of teaching, but we are offering insight into the *why* behind each particular decision as well.

WHAT *THINKING ALOUD* LOOKS LIKE

Sharing your thinking involves taking something that is normally an invisible process, and making it visible—or actually audible—to those around you. Whether it takes place off to the side in conversations between a teacher and coach, or right in front of the whole class, *thinking aloud* can have a big impact on learning for all involved.

Listen to Your Metacognitive Self

When it comes to *thinking aloud* as a coach, you might find yourself wondering what it could look or sound like or what kind of thinking you would possibly have to share. In order to figure this out, we have to start by listening to the metacognitive voice that's inside our head.

Simply put, metacognition is thinking about your thinking. Lai (2011) explains that it includes "knowledge about oneself as a learner and the factors that might impact performance, knowledge about strategies, and knowledge about when and why to use strategies" (p. 2). While this may seem like a cumbersome and unnatural process, being metacognitive is actually something that most of us are doing naturally all the time. However, capitalizing on this rich thinking and then using it in our coaching may take some practice. Mostly it involves slowing down and listening to that voice in your head; the one that we typically don't even notice is there chatting away. To help us do this, here are a few questions we can ask ourselves while we are in planning with teachers or co-teaching in their classrooms:

- What's going on right now that I need to take notice of?
- What am I going to do next?
- Why have I decided to do this?
- What do I hope or expect to be the outcome of my decision/action?

While it may seem forced and artificial at first, slowing down and asking yourself these questions will start to bring your metacognitive thinking to the surface. Then when the opportunity arises to share your thinking aloud, your metacognitive voice will come in loud and clear.

Let the Thinking Flow Both Ways

QR Code 6.1
Thinking Aloud During a Third-Grade Reading Lesson

http://qrs.ly/b659nv0

Student-centered coaching is a collaborative process. While effective coaches have a strong foundation in instructional practice, they are not experts who are coming in to fix the teachers or tell them how to do it the right way. Rather, coaching is meant to be a partnership between professionals who both bring a variety of experience, insights, and expertise to the table. With the coaching move *thinking aloud*, this means that sharing thinking should be a two-way street. This might seem awkward for a teacher at first (as it might be for the coach, too!). But with a lot of modeling from the coach and some simple prompting with "Tell me what you're thinking right now," teachers are typically eager to share their own thinking and to be seen as a valuable partner in the process.

Sometimes when a coach is sharing his or her thinking aloud, it happens in a more formal way as if to say, "I'm going to stop right now to tell you what I'm thinking because this feels like a teachable moment." But as both the teacher and coach become more comfortable with sharing their thinking with one another, it often takes on the form of a highly reflective conversation happening right there in class. Getting teachers to share their own thinking is a great way to encourage them to be more metacognitive and reflective about their practice—thinking carefully about the *what* and *why* of all of the decisions that they are making throughout any given lesson.

Share Your Own Thinking Instead of Giving Advice

Once you have tuned into the metacognitive voice inside your head, it can still take some work to shift from telling how to do something to thinking aloud. As a classroom teacher helping students understand a math problem like 2/5 + 1/4 = ?, the inclination is to either show students how to do it or to ask questions that will lead them down that same path. Yet modeling your own thinking sounds entirely different, as we can see in Figure 6.1. Sharing your knowledge about specific strategies and when, why, and how you choose to use them is definitely not the same as simply *telling* or *asking* students what to do.

Figure 6.1 Telling, Questioning, and Thinking Aloud

Telling Students What to Do	Asking Open-Ended Questions	Thinking Aloud
First, you have to find a common denominator. So you multiply 5 times 4 to get 20. Then . . .	What do you notice about the denominators? So what do you need to do first?	When I see a problem with fractions, the first thing I wonder about is the denominator. If I'm going to be adding or subtracting, I know that I am going to have to find a common denominator. So in this problem I notice . . .

This principle holds true even more so in a student-centered coaching model since we are coming from the standpoint of collaborator rather than expert. Therefore, while it may be tempting to advise a teacher what to do in a given situation, we can both build rapport and push teacher learning deeper by sharing our own thinking. Figure 6.2 shows how giving advice sounds different from thinking aloud when coaching.

When *thinking aloud*, we are talking in the first person about what we are actually thinking at that exact moment rather than advising a teacher on what we think he or she should be doing. This makes the coaching collaborative, respectful, and reflective.

Figure 6.2 Giving Advice vs. Thinking Aloud

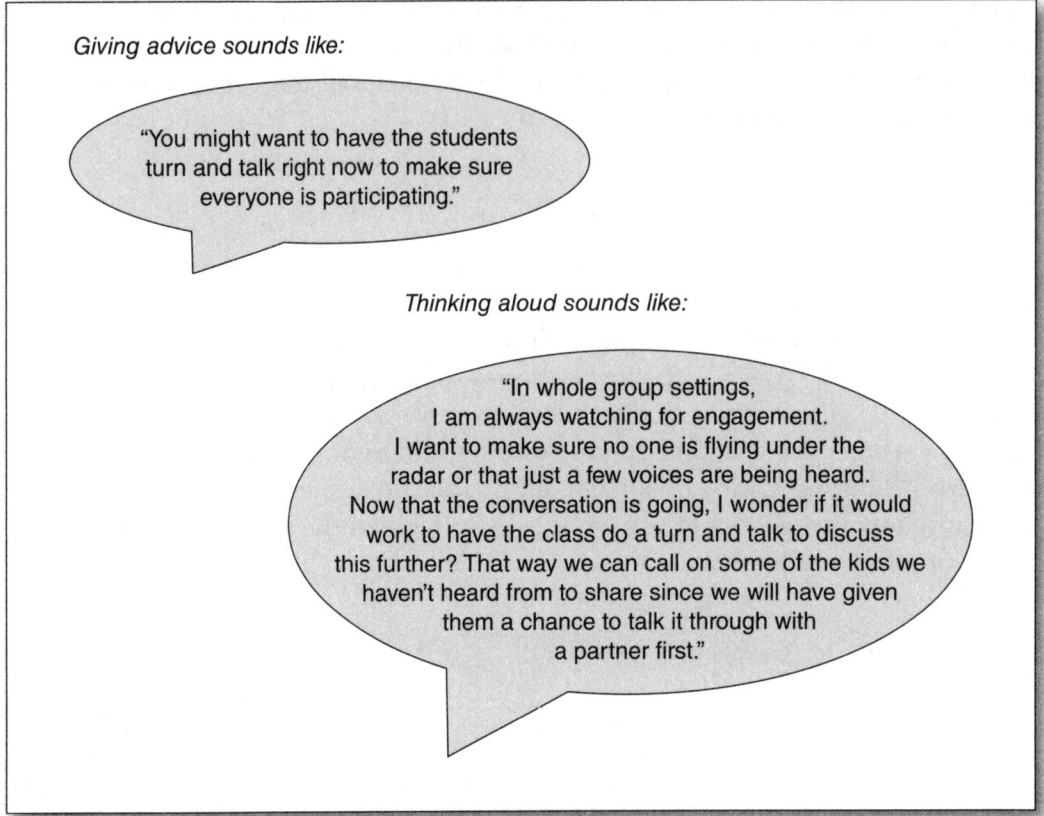

Show Students What It Means to be Metacognitive

Teachers often wonder if *thinking aloud* will be disruptive to their students. They worry that their second graders will lose track of the lesson if they stop with the coach to share their thinking, or they're afraid that their high school students will think it's silly to hear the adults in the room talking to each other in such a way. Although teachers are concerned that this coaching move could be a distraction to their students, *thinking aloud* can actually have a positive effect on learning. We know that being metacognitive enables us to be aware of when and why we employ certain strategies, and it is also how we monitor our understanding along the way. So when students have the opportunity to hear adults sharing their metacognitive processes aloud, they are being offered strong and authentic models of what it sounds like to think about your thinking.

Additionally, exposing students to this type of collaboration offers a very real way to walk our talk as learners. We expect our students to be active and engaged learners, but too often they don't see us the same way. When a coach and teacher share their thinking aloud, they are modeling that they, too, are constantly trying to figure it out and always working to get better at their craft. Students of all ages benefit from understanding that their teachers are not experts who have all the answers but rather people who are always seeking to learn and improve.

While modeling our metacognitive processes can be beneficial to students, keep in mind that not all thinking is fit to be shared aloud in front of the whole class. When referring to specific students, especially in the context of them not getting it or needing additional support, the thinking can be shared off to the side in hushed tones between the coach and teacher. Even in this scenario, the students will get the message that the coach and teacher are learning and collaborating together for the benefit of the class.

Share Your Thinking . . . as It Relates to the Goal

Since teaching involves making countless decisions in a given moment, it may be tempting to share thinking aloud about any number of things that are going on during a lesson. This was the case when Marco was in a coaching cycle with Elissa. The goal was for her first-grade students to write stories about a single topic with several sequential events and supporting details. Most of the students were emerging writers, and it was going to take a lot for them to reach this goal. From spending so much time in Elissa's class, Marco had also noticed that several of her students were reading below grade level. His passion was teaching reading, and it wasn't long before he saw his opening. Ivy and Jayden had finished working on their stories and were sitting on a beanbag taking turns reading to each other. Marco crouched down to listen for a few minutes and then went over to Elissa: "I was just listening to Ivy and Jayden read over there. They both seem to know a few sight words but were struggling with decoding any words they didn't already know. I'm wondering if you've noticed this with any of the other kids and if we should plan for some targeted phonics instruction." Elissa gave Marco a puzzled look and then said, "Um, sure. I guess we could talk about that when we meet tomorrow." She walked over to confer with one of her students on their writing and seemed to avoid Marco for the rest of the lesson.

It is important to remember, as we discussed in Chapter 1, that when a goal for students has been established as the focus for the coaching cycle, all of our coaching work should relate to that goal. In thinking aloud to Elissa about her students' reading (when her goal was writing),

QR Code 6.2
Thinking Aloud During Middle School Lessons

http://qrs.ly/vu59nv3

Shared goal + understanding

Marco was focusing on his agenda rather than honoring the goal she had set for her students. Within that goal there were many things about which he could share his thinking: the rigor and depth of student work, evidence of whether students were meeting the learning target, the quality of student discussions in giving each other feedback, or the pacing of the lesson. Instead, he shared thinking that wasn't relevant in the moment and even risked alienating the teacher he was supposed to be helping. When we stay within the focus agreed upon at the outset of the coaching cycle, we honor the goal set by the teacher and can still get the most out of this coaching move.

Think Aloud across all Parts of a Lesson

As with most coaching moves, *thinking aloud* can and should be used during all parts of a lesson. In whole group instruction, a coach might share his thinking about how to adjust instruction after doing a quick check for understanding with the class. While working with a small group, a teacher may share her thinking about what to do after she notices that several of the students still need more practice with a concept. And in conferring with an individual student, both the teacher and coach may share their thinking about what they are gleaning from listening to the student and how they will use this information to keep pushing student learning forward.

Kelly partnered with Randy on a coaching cycle in his high school genetics class. During the first few times in the class, Kelly's main focus was to collect student evidence. She and Randy both moved about the room after the whole group lesson to confer with kids and collect anecdotal notes. While this was helpful in planning for next steps in instruction, Kelly wondered if some opportunities for learning and reflection were being missed when they spent the whole lesson with different groups of students. For the next lesson, the students were going to be working toward the learning target, "I can identify each phase of mitosis in a plant cell." They would practice labeling the phases in a whole group lesson to start. The students who were ready would move on to a lab to identify the phases in an onion root, and those who still needed extra help would get small group support. To mix things up, Kelly suggested that this time she and Randy stick closer together so they could share their thinking with one another. Now, in addition to collecting student evidence, they could reflect upon and share their instructional decision making in the moment instead of waiting to talk about it at a later planning session. Figure 6.3 shows some examples of how their *thinking aloud* sounded in each part of the lesson.

As we can see from these examples, *thinking aloud* is a coaching move that can be used across grade levels, content areas, and instructional settings.

Figure 6.3 *Thinking Aloud* Across a Lesson

During whole group instruction:

Kelly: The same three kids are answering all of the questions. I'm thinking we should have them do the rest on their own and then compare with a partner.

Randy: I know they are all excited to get to the lab, but I see a few of the kids are just randomly guessing. Even though we want them to self-select where to go next, I think we should encourage a few kids to join the small group if they don't make that choice themselves.

During small group instruction:

Kelly: Enrique seems to get the concepts, but I'm wondering if language is getting in the way. What if you work on the vocabulary with him for a few minutes while I continue with the rest of the group?

Randy: Everyone gets the location of chromosomes, but they're not seeing the connection to the state of the nuclear membrane. I feel like I've run out of ways to explain it.

During individual instruction:

Kelly: I'm wondering what's next for Amelia. She totally gets this and whizzed through the lab. She can get started on the write-up for the rest of the period, but we're going to have to think about how to keep her challenged.

Randy: I notice that Derrick, Helena, and Victor are all getting confused between anaphase and metaphase. How about if we pull them together for a quick review.

Whether during whole group, small group, or one-on-one instruction, it provides a valuable tool to help reflect upon and make informed decisions in the moment that teaching and learning are happening.

LESSONS FROM THE FIELD

Heather had been in a coaching cycle with Leah, a fifth-grade teacher, for a few weeks. Their goal was for students to be able to read informational text and cite evidence to support their thinking. As a framework for their instruction, they were using the "signposts" identified

(Continued)

(Continued)

by Beers and Probst (2013) in the book *Notice and Note: Strategies for Close Reading*. Specifically, they were working with students to think about how the signposts transferred to informational text. As a whole class, they created an anchor chart that listed each of the signposts, and compared what it looked like in narrative text versus informational text. Since then, Beers and Probst (2015) have tackled this topic in the book *Reading Nonfiction*. But, at the time, it was uncharted territory that Heather and Leah were eager to explore.

When it was time for the students to apply this new strategy in their independent reading, they documented their thinking on a graphic organizer. In the first column, they identified a signpost, then they listed where in the text they noticed it, and lastly they shared their thinking. As the students fanned out around the room with text, graphic organizer, and pencil in hand, Heather suggested that they try sticking together to co-confer.

Part way through the lesson, the teacher and coach pulled up a chair and sat on either side of Max, who was reading an article on advancements in sports technique. Looking at Max's graphic organizer, they saw that he had identified the signpost "again and again." Leah asked Max to tell them about what he found and what he was thinking. He explained that the author gave several examples of baseball players who changed their batting stance and then saw an improvement in their hitting. Heather clarified, "Wow. So you're saying that the author used the signpost 'again and again' in a totally different way, by giving multiple examples, instead of by using a word or phrase over and over? That is some amazing thinking that you've done." Max confirmed with a nod of his head and a proud smile on his face.

At this point, Max ducked his head back into his reading while Leah and Heather pushed their chairs back to share their thinking, or to engage in what they call "teacher talk." Something big had just happened, and they were both eager to process it. The following conversation ensued:

Leah: I'm so excited about what Max has done. But I'm wondering if Max's case is really about comparing two things. Does this still fit with how we have defined the "contrast and contradictions" signpost for informational text? I'm not sure.

Heather: Are the different examples really about comparing? I don't know. Maybe at the end of class we have Max share what he found and how he thinks it applies to "again and again." Then we can talk with the kids about if they think perhaps his example could actually fit with both signposts. That could help clarify their thinking, too.

Leah: That sounds good, but I'm still wondering how "contrast and contradiction" works in informational texts myself. It's much less clear to me than the others.

Heather: I think we should see how it goes when Max shares with the whole class, and then you and I can also look for some more specific examples to try to figure it out for ourselves.

Leah is a very effective teacher and by nature highly reflective. She and Heather were working in a true partnership when they co-conferred and shared their thinking with one another. This took their reflection, and their own learning, to a level that perhaps neither could achieve on their own.

When they were done *thinking aloud*, Leah and Heather jotted down some notes from the conference and moved on to another student. In the sharing session, just as planned, Max told about his finding from the text, and they had a lively class discussion about the signpost "again and again." By taking the time to share their thinking with one another right there in the moment, Heather and Leah were able to process what had happened with Max, identify where there was still a lack of clarity, and create a game plan for the next step in instruction. Rather than telling Leah or giving her advice about what to do, they were both being highly reflective and working in partnership on the *what* and *why* of their instruction.

TOOLS AND TECHNIQUES

Troubleshooting Around Thinking Aloud

Slowing down your thinking and sharing it with someone else can feel awkward and even staged. Some things to consider if you find you're having trouble with this coaching move are listed in Figure 6.4.

Figure 6.4 Language for Thinking Aloud

If I'm thinking or finding . . .	Then I should remember that . . .
I'm working with a brand new teacher, and it seems like it would be helpful for me to just tell him what to do sometimes.	Most people don't learn by me doing the thinking and making the decisions for them. When I share my thinking aloud, I am modeling how to teach and giving him something to reflect on.
The teacher I'm working with worries that when I share my thinking aloud to her the students think we're talking about them.	It's actually beneficial to students to know what the teacher and I are doing when we talk together in quiet voices during class time. Being metacognitive is a practice that we want all students to be engaged in, so in *thinking aloud* with a teacher we are providing them with an excellent model.
I don't even know if the thinking I'm sharing with the teacher makes sense or is what's best for the students!	As with any coaching move, this is not about being the expert or having all the right answers. Rather the emphasis is on collaboration and modeling the importance of being reflective and thoughtful in my teaching practice.

Stems for Thinking Aloud

The following stems will help you get started with using the coaching move *thinking aloud*. After some practice, the language and practices will start to come naturally.

- Right now I'm thinking it would make sense to . . .
- I noticed . . . so I think we should . . .
- I think we might want to . . .
- I'm wondering about . . .
- Maybe we should consider . . .
- When I see . . . it makes me think . . .

A FINAL THOUGHT

Teaching is a complex process that involves countless decisions to be made on the spot during any given lesson. Most of these decisions are made in just a few seconds and entirely within the privacy of our own heads. It certainly would be helpful if there was an amazing machine that let us look into the thought process of another person in order to create insight into how and why we make such instructional choices. But since no such apparatus exists as of yet (except in perhaps some B-level sci-fi movie), we need to make our thinking visible by sharing it aloud. Just like we do with our students when helping them understand how to use comprehension strategies or how to take on a challenging math problem or even how to drive.

Thinking aloud allows us to take advantage of learning opportunities as they happen, model being a reflective thinker and learner, and work in a collaborative manner with teachers. It is fun to spend time in this metacognitive space and reflect alongside teachers. And if we do it in an open-minded fashion, it relieves any pressure of feeling evaluative or judgmental of teachers. We are right there, by the teacher's side, supporting student learning. While it may take some getting used to, *thinking aloud* is an important and valuable tool to have in our coaching toolkit.

7 Sorting Student Work

Mt. Sherman is one of Colorado's fifty-three peaks that rise above 14,000 feet in elevation, and it sits just outside of the old mining town of Leadville. Hiking at this altitude is a unique and exciting experience. Setting off just before dawn, you are greeted by amazing fields of wildflowers just as the sun begins to rise. As you start to climb above the tree line, the trail crosses multiple scree fields, or giant patches of large rocks. As you gain elevation, the high-alpine vegetation gets smaller and smaller due to the limited oxygen available at such heights. Sighting tiny flowers with their delicate leaves is one of the special treats of hiking peaks such as this.

After reaching the summit and making the long descent back to the trailhead, you can turn around to admire your accomplishment. A majestic bald peak stands in front of you, which you weren't able to appreciate in its entirety when you began the predawn ascent. Now in full light, you can just make out the trail that zigzags up the steep slope to the summit. The scree fields look like little more than dirt patches off in the distance, but now you know better. It is a sight to behold!

If you happen to be flying from Denver to points west, you can appreciate Mt. Sherman in an entirely different way—from the window of an airplane. You certainly can't make out any of the details, but you get a wonderful perspective of the peak as it sits in the Mosquito Range of the Rocky Mountains. You see the big contours and drainages that lead to nearby valleys. It is yet another way to understand such a special place.

When thinking about how we use student data to drive instruction, we can also consider the different vantage points from which we sit. Many data discussions happen at the airplane window view where we become aware of how our school or district sits within a larger context. You can't make out details, but you can see bigger patterns and trends. Within our schools, we often have data discussions at the level of the whole mountain view. We talk about grade level and schoolwide performance, often in the form of spreadsheets and percentages. In our coaching cycles, we look at data on the ground level. Just like out on the trail, we want to take notice of every rock and flower. As with the intimate view we get while hiking, when we look carefully at student evidence, it helps us understand the needs and nuances of each individual student. It is at this up-close vantage point where the coaching move *sorting student work* sits.

THE MOVE—*SORTING STUDENT WORK*

As we've discussed throughout this book, student-centered coaching depends on using student evidence to plan instruction. One of our favorite coaching moves is to sort student work with teachers because it is a productive way to help teachers see—and act upon—the different needs of students in their classrooms. *Sorting student work* is used throughout the coaching cycle. At the beginning of the cycle, we sort student work to collect baseline data. Throughout the cycle, we sort student work to make daily instructional decisions. At the end of the cycle, we sort a post-assessment to determine who has met the goal and make follow-up plans for any students who haven't.

When *sorting student work*, a teacher or team of teachers sits down with the coach and a pile of student work and sorts that work against a clear learning target or set of success criteria. By analyzing the work in such a way, teachers and their coach can gain insight into where students are in relation to the daily target or the larger goal for learning. They can collect baseline data, create groups for differentiated instruction, or confirm whether or not the class is ready to move on to the next step.

WHY *SORTING STUDENT WORK* IS IMPORTANT

There is a lot of talk in education around the importance of formative assessment. There are also varying interpretations of what that term actually means. Dylan Wiliam (2011) states, "An assessment functions formatively to the extent that evidence about student achievement is elicited, interpreted, and used by teachers, learners or their peers to make decisions about the next steps in instruction" (p. 43). So far we have identified several places within the framework for student-centered coaching where we assess formatively—when pre-assessing at the beginning of a coaching cycle and when using the coaching moves *noticing and naming* and *thinking aloud* in the classroom. In this chapter, we focus on formative assessment through *sorting student work*.

In the book, *Student-Centered Coaching at the Secondary Level,* Diane (Sweeney, 2013) explains the value in coaching teachers to shift from a "deliver and assess" approach to "assess and deliver." This is also referred to as the "teaching and learning cycle," where we continually look at student evidence to plan for what students need next. In approaching instruction this way, we "often find the need to differentiate learning based on the students' needs, because on any given day in any given classroom, the students are in different places as learners" (p. 42). When we sit with a teacher or team after a lesson to sort through the evidence we've collected, we can make decisions based on where we *know* the students are instead of on simply what comes next in the curriculum guide. This allows us to assess formatively and then plan instruction in a way that is responsive to the needs of all the students in the classroom.

Teachers often share with coaches that they experience a sense of dread or extra stress because they don't feel they have time to go through piles of tests or other assignments for every class every day. Teaching is a tough enough job as is, and adding to the stress is certainly not the intent of this coaching move. We are careful to be thoughtful about the kind of evidence we are collecting and how we are using it, so that teachers start to see this coaching practice as much more relevant to their day-to-day work than just getting the whole mountain or airplane view. This can make a big impact on student achievement.

WHAT *SORTING STUDENT WORK* LOOKS LIKE

Sorting student work occurs primarily when we co-plan lessons with teachers. Throughout our coaching cycles, we regularly put all of the work out on the table and go through it in a systematic way to look for trends, determine needs-based groups, and make decisions about what to teach next. We use a variety of tools and strategies to keep the conversation focused on the work that is in front of us.

QR Code 7.1

Analyzing Student Work–Twelfth Grade

http://qrs.ly/ez59nva

Start by Thinking Broadly About Data

In today's educational climate, *data* is a very loaded word. There are data teams, data walls, and data-driven instruction, and we view much of this data as being limited to tests. These tests are commonly mandated at the district or state level, with results that can be aggregated and disaggregated—through spreadsheets, graphs, and percentages. *Data*, therefore, often become the source of stress, frustration, and even political debate. Educators report having loads of data but not really knowing how to effectively use it.

Looking at quantitative data can be useful to identify school or district-wide trends and achievement gaps and to set big-picture goals. But when thinking about partnering with teachers through student-centered coaching, we need use an entirely different type of data. We are looking for student evidence that we can collect *today* and that will inform us about what our students need *tomorrow*. So instead of looking at spreadsheets from big formal tests, we look at things like student writing samples, math problems, exit slips, and responses to reading. In this way, we can gain an understanding of where students are in relation to that day's learning and plan for next steps in instruction moving forward.

Focus on Evidence That Is Descriptive and Aligned

Tasha was working with her coach Elisa in a coaching cycle focused on third-grade subtraction. They were interested in using more student data to drive their instructional decisions, which was also a schoolwide goal. A few weeks into their collaboration, they decided that they needed some evidence of how the kids were doing, so they gave the students the mid-unit quiz from the district math curriculum. The assessment was comprised mostly of multiple-choice questions, so it didn't take too long for Tasha to grade. When she finished, she tallied all of the results in a spreadsheet, and Elisa came in during their scheduled planning time to discuss next steps. However, their discussion yielded more questions than answers. Why did so many students get one particular problem correct and a similar problem wrong? Did all of the problems relate to what they had taught? Where were the breakdowns in understanding? How could the results help them to differentiate instruction? Not quite sure how to use the data they had in front of them, Elisa suggested they continue on with the next lesson and perhaps give another quiz the following week.

It's no surprise that Tasha and Elisa's process was less than useful. What they had selected as a formative assessment didn't go very far in surfacing the students' understandings. For this reason, this is not the kind of student evidence that we find to be most beneficial during our coaching cycles.

In order for the student evidence to be useful, it must allow us to see what students know and understand, or to make their thinking *visible*. If all we know about a particular student is that she got 70 percent of the questions right on a subtraction quiz, we can only guess what it will take in order to keep moving her learning forward. In this case, the natural assumption is that she simply needs more practice with her math facts. However, if we can see in her work that she still doesn't understand the conceptual underpinnings of subtraction, then we know that she doesn't have other strategies to fall back on when she doesn't know the facts. With more descriptive evidence, we can plan to support her in a targeted and meaningful way.

Additionally, we need to make sure that the evidence we're gathering is aligned to the learning targets. Just like Sue, the high school science teacher we read about in Chapter 2, if we end up with a bunch of evidence that isn't directly related to the intended learning, it's not going to be of much use to us. When planning for a particular lesson, we want to ask, "What evidence are we going to collect to see if they have met the day's learning target?" If it's both descriptive and aligned, the data we collect will be very useful for planning.

Several months passed, and Tasha and Elisa were collaborating in a coaching cycle on multiplication. After a lot of trial and error, they started to design exit tickets that do a better job of making the students' learning visible (Figure 7.1). They did this by giving students the opportunity to show their math thinking in one or two problems that are directly tied to the day's learning target and then reflect on where they feel they are in relation to that target. These quick little exercises packed a powerful punch in yielding a goldmine of data for Tasha and Elisa to use in planning next steps. As Doug Lemov (2010) points out in *Teach Like a Champion*, using exit tickets like these will "ensure that you always check for understanding in

Figure 7.1 Exit Ticket From Tasha's Third-Grade Math Class

Learning Target: I can create real-world stories to demonstrate my understanding of multiplication.

Write a story that represents 7 x 5. Draw a picture that explains your thinking.

There are 7 trees and 5 apples on each tree. How many apples are there?

Did you meet the learning target? How do you know?

I met the target because I know that 7 x 5 = 35, and my drawing shows 35 apples.

a way that provides you with strong data and thus critical insights. . . . What mistake did those who got it wrong make? Why, in looking at their errors, did they make that mistake? What about your lesson might have led to that confusion?" (p. 106). When the evidence we collect is both descriptive and aligned, it makes *sorting student work* a highly productive coaching move.

Collect Evidence That Is Efficient— for Both Students and Teachers

Leanna was recently checking in with some coaches she has been working with. Their district had just launched a new coaching initiative, and everyone was jumping into their first round of coaching cycles. When she asked Ken, a middle school coach, how it was going, he reported, "We gave the social studies unit pretest last week but are only about half way through the grading. I'm hoping we can start sorting them and plan instruction by next Monday." While Ken was certainly on the right track in terms of collecting baseline data to use with the teacher to plan for the unit, Leanna couldn't help but wonder how useful the information would still be once they finally got to it or how sustainable this practice would seem to the teacher at that point in time.

In reflecting on the situation that afternoon, the team of coaches discussed the need for evidence collected to be *efficient* in every way. First, this means that teachers and coaches should either collect work that the students are already doing in class or generate things like pretests, exit tickets, and quizzes that don't take an entire planning period to create. Second, they should be sure that the work they ask students to do is authentic or at least doesn't take up a lot of extra class time to complete (as in the case of an exit ticket or quiz). Finally, they should collect evidence that can be analyzed and sorted in a short amount of time. Lengthy written assignments, projects, and end-of-unit tests all have their place in classroom teaching. But when thinking about *sorting student work* to plan for instruction in the short term, this group of coaches quickly realized that less time creating, generating, and analyzing is the way to go to make this an effective and sustainable practice.

Consider When to Use Sorting Sessions

The move *sorting student work* is one of the strategies that are used by teachers and coaches to formatively assess student learning in order to gain clarity about where they are in relation to the intended learning. Sometimes we do this as instruction occurs. On other occasions, our evidence is more anecdotal, such as with conference notes. We have found that when we sort conference notes, we may highlight trends or trace how students perform from week to week. This may feel a little bit different from a sorting session in which a teacher and coach make piles of student work.

Coaches may also use *sorting sessions* as a vehicle for planning an overall unit of study. We can set up checkpoints across a unit of study at the outset. This way we are ready at certain points to do a deeper analysis and reflection on how students are performing in comparison to the unit objectives as a whole.

While there is no magic number of times per week that evidence should be collected to sort, it would be unrealistic to expect to be doing it every day for every subject or class taught. Rather, it should be thoughtfully built into the mix of the many ways we formatively assess students—whether during or after class. Figure 7.2 includes examples of some the types of student work that we use and when in the process we might be sorting.

QR Code 7.2
Sorting and Planning From Student Work, Secondary

http://qrs.ly/h459nv6

Figure 7.2 Examples of *Sorting Student Work*

Before the lesson:
- Pre-assessments at the beginning of a unit of study

During the lesson:
- Entrance tickets
- Warm-ups
- Checks for understanding from whiteboards or technological platforms such as *Plickr* or *Kahoot*
- Conference notes

At the end of the lesson:
- Quizzes
- Exit tickets
- Classwork
- Post-assessments at the end of the unit of study

Sort Student Work With Teams of Teachers

Analyzing student work with teams of teachers is certainly not a new concept. Many schools have had built-in structures for data teams and professional learning communities (PLCs). The difference is these data-driven conversations often focus on analyzing reading levels or test data from across a team or grade level. We prefer to use student work as a driver of planning.

QR Code 7.3

Sorting Student Work With a First-Grade Team

http://qrs.ly/ xu59nv7

Team dynamics can easily affect these conversations, so we are careful to avoid situations when a team may go through the motions rather than dig deep into the work that is in front of them. For example, we have found that each teacher bringing a single piece of student work creates a situation where there is a high level of subjectivity to the work that is chosen. Teachers may not want to acknowledge that many of their students didn't perform well on a given assignment or exit ticket and therefore just grab the one that is the strongest, therefore missing out on a rich learning opportunity. Or their own natural biases about students may seep in: "Keisha is always at the top of the class so I'll be sure to bring in her work." We have also found that if everyone in the group is only looking at their own students' work, we lose the chance to have fresh eyes examining our kids' work and possibly breaking down some of our preconceived notions about them. And when there are too many pieces of student evidence to analyze, the process can feel cumbersome and unproductive.

As you will see in the following example, we have found that when a team of teachers and their coach look at one complete class set of work to analyze and sort, it becomes a rich, collaborative, and productive learning experience for the whole team. Together they look for trends in the work and surface needs for whole class and small group instruction. The expectation is that in doing all the heavy lifting together around one set of students' work, the other teachers can quickly go through and sort their own piles based on the shared conclusions drawn by the group.

LESSONS FROM THE FIELD

Julia, Scott, and Amelia are a tight-knit seventh-grade language arts team. In trying to catch up to their new state standards, they were trying to use more informational text. Since this was not a totally comfortable area for any of them, they decided to approach the school's instructional coach, Josh, for help.

After some time dissecting the standards, Josh and the team came up with the goal "Students will compare and contrast across multiple texts and use evidence to support their thinking." In discussing what success would look like with this goal, they created the following learning targets:

- I can annotate in order to make meaning from the text.
- I can identify the main idea of more than one informational text.
- I can develop a theory of how a few texts work together to frame a broader idea.
- I can use textual evidence to support my thinking.
- I can clearly articulate my thinking in writing.
- I can include relevant information in my writing.

To collect baseline data, the team pulled two short texts and a writing prompt that matched the success criteria. Josh worked with the teachers to score their class samples against each of the targets on a four-point scale, with 1 being just beginning and 4 exceeding the expectation. It wasn't a surprise that many of the students weren't there yet. But some were further along than they expected. In fact, there was a fair amount of evidence that the students were able to annotate and synthesize a single text. Where they needed help was putting the two texts together. Figuring this out gave the teachers a new perspective about what to focus on in their lessons.

While the team was able to work with several learning targets at one time, we sometimes find that this can be tricky because there is so much to think about. When this is the case, we scale it back and prioritize just a few learning targets to work with. For example, they could have only paid attention to how the students approached annotation or providing evidence. This may have allowed them to go deeper in their analysis of a few learning targets. But since the team was just beginning the unit, they elected to look at all of the learning targets to get a broad-based view of student performance.

After reviewing the student work, Amelia suggested that they use the book *A Long Walk to Water* by Linda Sue Park (2010) as a starting point. The book is based on the true story of Salvo, one of the "Lost Boys" of Sudan from the Nuer tribe, and includes a parallel story of a young girl, Nya, of the Dinko tribe. They also found an article about the modern conflict that has ensued between these tribes in Sudan. With these two rich texts at hand, Josh and the teachers dug into instruction that addressed the learning targets.

Throughout the unit, the teachers collected evidence to guide their instruction. This included anecdotal conference notes and class work that the students did to track their thinking. After a few weeks, they decided to do a more substantial check-in to see if the students

(Continued)

(Continued)

could start putting all the pieces together into writing. Since they had built up a solid base of knowledge from the two texts that they had explored, the team decided to try another writing prompt. This time it was "What are some similar and different perspectives of the people of the Dinko and Nuer tribes?" Students were reminded to use evidence from the two texts to support their thinking and include at least one quote to serve as evidence.

The next morning, they met to look at the students' writing samples. Whereas up until now they had tried to look at everyone's student work at once, Josh suggested with this longer piece that they look deeply at just one teacher's class set. He came prepared with a copy of Scott's class set for himself and each of the teachers. He also wrote all of the learning targets on the board. The group chose to use a protocol to guide them through the sorting session (see Figure 7.3). They each grabbed a pile of sticky notes and got busy reading and looking for themes.

Once they finished reading the student work, Josh opened up the discussion: "So what are you noticing?" Julia jumped in: "I think all of our work on analyzing the text has really paid off. It seems like everyone was able to give examples of how the two tribes are similar and different." "Except for maybe Jeffrey and Ana," Amelia said. "I think the two of them weren't really able to state the examples clearly." Julia

Figure 7.3 Protocol for Sorting Student Work

1. If possible, make a copy of the set of class work for each participant. Otherwise, make fewer copies for participants to examine in pairs. Alternatively, the work can be divided among the group, and participants can write comments on sticky notes before passing their stack to the next person.
2. Read through the entire set of class work, looking for trends relative to the learning targets.
3. Discuss the trends that were noticed. Collectively, decide which ones are the most significant and need further instruction—either whole or small group.
4. Go back to the work to sort students according to the identified needs. If something pertains to the whole class, this will be addressed in whole group instruction.
5. Plan for instruction based on the needs of each group.

said she thought there may be a few others, too. Scott explained that with Ana it might be a language issue. They discussed how he could follow up with her independently.

"What stuck out to me is that I need to do more explicit instruction around stating a clear point," Scott said. "The kids were all over the board with their openings, which makes me think they don't even know what that should look like."

As the discussion continued, the group shared a few more trends. Some students were still struggling to integrate relevant evidence from the text into their writing. Some were just quoting the text verbatim when they should have been paraphrasing, and all but three students still needed work on explaining how the quote they chose supports their point.

With all of the trends identified, Josh summarized their thinking, "The two things we need to address in whole group instruction are stating a clear main point and explaining how their quote supports that point. And for small groups we can address some of the other learning targets. Does that sound alright?" The team nodded in affirmation. They were ready to go back into the work to sort students into groups. But Scott hesitated: "I'm just wondering about Jeffrey. I know I need to work with him on providing evidence, and in reality, he could stand to be in each one of these groups. This is where I get so overwhelmed at the thought of differentiated instruction. What do you do with those kids who realistically need to be in three or four groups?" Everyone could identify with Scott's concern, and a few minutes of thoughtful discussion followed. In the end, they concluded that sometimes you just have to think about a student's biggest need and start there. Fortunately, these concepts are continually revisited across different subjects and grade levels. Josh reminded everyone that in getting to know students so well through this process, teachers can always be on the lookout for other opportunities to support their individual learning needs.

The team spent the last few minutes of the planning period sorting the students' work. Since this was a more involved set of student work than what they normally look at, they didn't have time left to dig into planning. So they decided to table that until the next day. Julia and Amelia would take each of their class sets and group students according to the needs they had identified from Scott's kids. Because they planned and taught so closely together, they were confident that their classes would follow roughly the same trends.

(Continued)

> (Continued)
>
> By *sorting student work*, Josh and the seventh-grade team had created an efficient assessment that was directly tied to the learning targets. Using the protocol helped them analyze the student work in a structured format that enabled them to identify trends and ultimately the specific needs of each student. Their thoughtful collaboration demonstrates the power of *sorting student work* as a highly informative and impactful coaching move.

TOOLS AND TECHNIQUES

Troubleshooting Around Sorting Student Work

While an important and productive practice, *sorting student work* can initially seem challenging and even intimidating. Figure 7.4 provides language to help work through problems or concerns that may arise.

Figure 7.4 Language for Sorting Student Work

If I hear . . .	Then I can use the following language . . .
I don't have time to create and grade a new test every other day to see how my kids are doing.	We want to collect student evidence that is authentic and easy to analyze. Why don't we start by taking a look at the work they've done in class today and see what we can learn from it?
I know my students really well and don't need to gather any specific evidence to know what they need.	I can tell how hard you work to know each one of your students. But if we collect actual evidence—even if it's anecdotal—we can look through it together to find trends and needs that we might not otherwise be able to catch.
It feels like a waste of my time to look through another teacher's student work. I'm not sure how that would help me and my own students.	Having multiple sets of eyes on the same set of student work really creates some rich learning opportunities for everyone and helps us calibrate our understandings and expectations as a team of what success looks like and how to meet students' needs. Usually what you find in your teammate's class will apply directly to your own students as well, so you won't need to go through the whole process again.

Four Square Planner

When *sorting student work*, it is helpful to have a system to keep track of who will go in which group and what the instructional focus will be. This graphic organizer, which we call the "four square planner," enables a teacher and coach to easily keep track of students while sorting their work. There is space to plan for whole group instruction and to identify and plan for up to four differentiated groups (see Figure 7.5).

Figure 7.5 Four Square Planner

Whole Group Instruction:	
Focus of Instruction: Students:	Focus of Instruction: Students:
Focus of Instruction: Students:	Focus of Instruction: Students:

Checklist for Collecting Student Evidence

Throughout the chapter, we have discussed several criteria to consider when planning for *sorting student work* (see Figure 7.6).

Figure 7.6 Checklist for Collecting Student Evidence

- It doesn't take long to create.
- It doesn't require a lot of class time for students to produce (or is simply work they are already doing in class).
- It can be analyzed as part of regular planning time.
- It is aligned with standard(s) and learning target(s).
- It makes thinking visible.
- It doesn't leave much room for guessing such as with yes/no or true/false.

A FINAL THOUGHT

As teachers, we often finish a lesson with what seems like an innate sense of whether the students got it or not. Occasionally we go back and reteach things based on what we *think* students need. And sometimes, with the pressure of pacing guides and covering curriculum, we feel that we ought to move on regardless. It is only through the analysis of student work that we can truly *know* what students did or did not learn from a given lesson. With this up-close view we can direct instruction to target students' specific needs.

Out on the mountain, we can gain an amazing understanding of our surroundings as we appreciate the details of the different types of rocks, flowers, trees, and the steep rise of the trail. When coaches engage in *sorting student work* with a teacher or team, they are helping to create opportunities for teachers to understand their students' different needs in a similarly up-close and meaningful way.

8 Providing Strengths-Based Feedback

In her bestselling book *Daring Greatly*, Brené Brown (2012) writes, "There's no question that feedback may be one of the most difficult arenas to negotiate in our lives. We should remember, though, that victory is not getting good feedback, avoiding giving difficult feedback, or avoiding the need for feedback. Instead, it's taking off the armor, showing up, and engaging" (p. 206). We couldn't agree more. Yet, while we know that feedback is essential to learning, it's never been easy terrain for us to navigate in our coaching. Do we seek to provide warm and cool feedback and hope that it goes over well? Do we stick with feedback that is specific to student learning in the effort to stay student-centered? Or do we find a more meaningful way to embed feedback into our coaching work?

Asking ourselves these questions led us to the book *Coaching Conversations: Transforming Your School One Conversation at a Time* (Cheliotes & Reilly, 2010, p. 67). The authors suggest a framework for providing what they call "reflective feedback" using the following process:

1. Clarifying questions or statements

2. Value statements or questions

3. Questions or possibility statements

After years of feeling unsure about how to provide feedback, this framework felt like salvation. We could do this. We finally had a vision for how to provide feedback without jeopardizing our relationships or feeling like we were in an evaluative (or fixing) role. Our new vision meant that feedback, like every other part of our coaching work, could be based on partnerships wherein the coach and teacher work together to reach their goals for student learning.

THE MOVE—*PROVIDING STRENGTHS-BASED FEEDBACK*

The research regarding feedback is clear. It is essential for learning to occur. Without feedback, the learner is unclear about the steps to take to improve. With feedback, there is a clear vision for what the learner can do to move their learning forward. Engaged learners wonder, "If this is where I'm headed, then how am I doing on my journey to get there?" This is when feedback becomes critical to learning.

Providing strengths-based feedback occurs as the teacher and coach work together to implement instructional practices. Without feedback, teachers are less able to modify their instruction to meet the needs of their students. Working from strengths is part of fostering coaching relationships that are trusting, respectful, and productive. Brené Brown (2012) writes, "In my experience, the heart of valuable feedback is taking the 'strengths perspective.' Viewing performance from the strengths perspective offers us the opportunity to examine our struggles in light of our capacities, talents, competencies, possibilities, visions, values, and hopes" (p. 199). We believe that *providing strengths-based feedback* enables us to engage with teachers in a way that honors the work they're doing while helping them grow as learners.

WHY *PROVIDING STRENGTHS-BASED FEEDBACK* IS IMPORTANT

The power of feedback became clear to Diane on the ski slopes of Colorado. In *Student-Centered Coaching at the Secondary Level* (Sweeney, 2013), she shared her journey to learn to telemark ski. Telemark skiing is known as *free heel skiing*, because the skier's heel isn't connected to the binding of the ski, which means the turn is exactly the opposite of regular skiing. Taking on this new learning provided insights into what it feels like to be an absolute novice.

Having skied for over thirty years on alpine skis didn't make the learning any easier. It was painfully obvious that she didn't look pretty as she made her way down the slope. She felt unsure and unsteady. She even asked her husband to film her because she thought that if she could see herself in action, then she would be able to improve more quickly. But later, as she watched the clip, Diane was confirmed in her suspicions that she looked silly. Her upper body moved to and fro in a spastic way. Her arms were flailing. Her stance looked odd. She realized that while she could see what was wrong, she had no idea how to make it right.

A few weeks later, Diane ran into some friends on the mountain. Jeff and Angela are both expert telemark skiers, and just as Diane was about to hang up her gear, they wouldn't let that happen. Instead they provided the feedback that she so desperately needed.

While making her way down the hill, Diane hardly noticed them watching her turns. When she arrived at the bottom, panting and out of breath, Jeff said, "You know, you are dragging your right ski pole. That's throwing off your balance." Angela added, "Yeah, if you pick up that pole, your balance will improve. Think about it like you're sitting on an exercise ball. That's where you want your weight to be."

Finally, Diane had something tangible that she could practice. On the next run she kept thinking about their advice and even chanted "exercise ball, exercise ball" as she skied down the hill. Gradually, she found herself able to pull the pole off the snow and stay in balance. Having this simple bit of feedback was just what Diane needed to fast-track her learning.

Jeff and Angela aren't educators, but they are teachers. They were able to teach Diane through the use of feedback that was timely and specific. They were able to move her learning forward.

WHAT *PROVIDING STRENGTHS-BASED FEEDBACK* LOOKS LIKE

There is a paradox at play when it comes to the role of feedback in our schools. Thanks to the recent emphasis on teacher evaluation, teachers are receiving more feedback than ever. Yet, many will tell you that they are feedback deprived. This tension is well-described in the recent book by Douglas Stone and Sheila Heen (2015) titled *Thanks for the Feedback: The Science and Art of Receiving Feedback Well.* Stone and Heen write, "Broadly, feedback comes in three forms: appreciation (thanks), coaching (here's a better way to do it), and evaluation (here's where you stand)" (p. 18.) Teachers seem to be receiving more than enough evaluative feedback and some appreciation (if they're lucky). What's missing is feedback that would be considered coaching. Here's what *providing strengths-based feedback* looks like when it is nested within a student-centered coaching cycle.

**QR Code 8.1
Providing Strengths-Based Feedback Within a Planning Session, High School Social Studies**

http://qrs.ly/iw59nvd

1. Clarify, 2. Value, and 3. Uncover Possibilities

Moving through these steps sets a coach up to provide feedback that honors the relationship and also helps the teacher learn and grow. Diane recently experienced this when working with a coach in a small Midwestern school district. Cindy requested direct feedback about her coaching. She said, "I don't want to miss anything. I want to be sure I'm doing a good job and could really use some feedback." In the past, this request would have made Diane nervous because she hadn't become comfortable in the art of providing feedback. Most likely some form of praise or conciliatory feedback would have been her first response. But she wanted to provide what Cindy needed, so she used the three steps as a mental framework for moving through the conversation. She began by probing Cindy to learn more about what she had tried, what was working, and where she was stuck (clarify). Then she honored the risks that Cindy was taking in putting herself out there as a coach and a learner (value). Then she brainstormed with Cindy to determine some next steps that would take her work further (uncover possibilities).

We like to think of that last step as the "and" phase of feedback. It's about thinking broadly and open mindedly about the possibilities of where to go next, rather than slipping in a "but" and hoping that the teacher doesn't notice. Feedback that is based on the "but" may sound like this: "Your students were engaged throughout the lesson, but I noticed that you mostly called on the boys." The "but" serves as a verbal eraser. It erases everything that came before it, and the teacher only hears, "I noticed that you mostly called on the boys." Using "and" opens new avenues of learning rather than shutting them down.

Relate Feedback to the Learning Targets

In Chapter 2, you read about using student-friendly learning targets during a coaching cycle. Learning targets ground coaching in the content and provide clarity around what we want the students to know and be able to do. When lessons are designed with high quality learning targets at the center, it becomes much easier for a coach to ground feedback in actual student performance, rather than on assumptions about what we think they can or cannot do. Figure 8.1 introduces how we can use the three steps for strengths-based feedback in a way that directly embeds learning targets.

Figure 8.1 The Connection Between Strengths-Based Feedback and the Learning Targets

Steps for Strengths-Based Feedback	Coaching Move	Language
1. Clarify	• Compare student evidence with the learning targets. • Discuss the instructional practices that supported student learning. • Reflect on how the lesson went, and discuss any questions that the teacher or coach may have.	• How are the students doing? • What did we do to make that happen? • What are you wondering about the lesson?
2. Value	• Celebrate examples of students who are meeting the learning targets. • Name the instructional practices that made an impact on student learning. • Identify what the students are doing well, and who may not be meeting the learning targets.	• Here's some evidence of student growth . . . • Here's what may have gotten us there . . . • Who are some specific students who nailed it? Who are we worried about?
3. Uncover Possibilities	• Plan future lessons based on the learning targets. • Discuss teaching practices that may support student learning. • Determine how learning will be scaffolded for those who are struggling or advanced.	• What can we do next? • How will this support student learning? • How will we differentiate?

Stay Focused on What the Teacher Has Committed to Learning and Doing

Hidden agendas, mixed messages, and judgmental thinking are off limits when it comes to *providing strengths-based feedback*. This may take some discipline, because we are often tempted to inject feedback that is based on what we think a teacher *should* be doing. Using this approach prevents a coach from getting traction because when it comes down to it, the teacher is the one who has to see the feedback through to action. If the teacher feels under attack, then he or she is far less likely to do so.

One of the most common methods we see coaches using is observing teachers and then following up with feedback. This often means that the coach sits in a corner of the classroom,

QR Code 8.2 Providing Strengths-Based Feedback at the End of a Sixth-Grade Coaching Cycle

http://qrs.ly/kx59nve

typing away as the teacher goes about teaching a lesson. Later, the coach tries to share what he or she noticed in a way that doesn't hurt the teacher's feelings or jeopardize their relationship. This couldn't be further from how we define the notion of *providing strengths-based feedback* because coaching in this way comes dangerously close to evaluation. After all, what do evaluators do? They sit in the back of the classroom, typing away as the teacher goes about teaching the lesson.

We believe in honoring teachers as learners, so we keep feedback focused on what they would like to accomplish. If the feedback isn't aligned with their goals, then we shouldn't be surprised if it doesn't go anywhere.

Provide More Than Praise

We'd probably agree that saying "Good job" wouldn't be considered giving high quality feedback to students. The same goes for working with adult learners. If we settle for praise rather than feedback, then we sell coaching short. What all learners need is feedback, and when we only provide praise, we miss opportunities for growth.

The tendency to provide praise as a form of feedback is common when coaching veteran teachers. The coach may be wondering, "How can I even begin to provide feedback to this master teacher?" Yet, even the most experienced teachers benefit from the three steps that make up strengths-based feedback.

A common pitfall is when coaches aren't spending enough time in classrooms alongside teachers. When this is the case, they may default to praise because feedback requires having a detailed understanding of what is going well and some options for where to go next. Being in the classroom is the only way for a coach to have the necessary context to *provide strengths-based feedback*.

Avoid Overwhelming the Teacher

One of the most enduring concepts of educational research is the Zone of Proximal Development, introduced by Lev Vygotsky. Vygotsky (1978) defines the Zone of Proximal Development (ZPD) as the space between what the learner can do unaided and what the learner cannot do (see Figure 8.2). It is the sweet spot where learning is properly scaffolded. While the ZPD originated as a construct for the learning that our students are engaged in, it also applies to adult learners. We have found that there is no use overwhelming teachers with a thousand suggestions. If we do so, then we are focusing entirely on the outer ring, or what the learner cannot do. As coaches, this is a first-class ticket to frustrating teachers or creating

Figure 8.2 Zone of Proximal Development

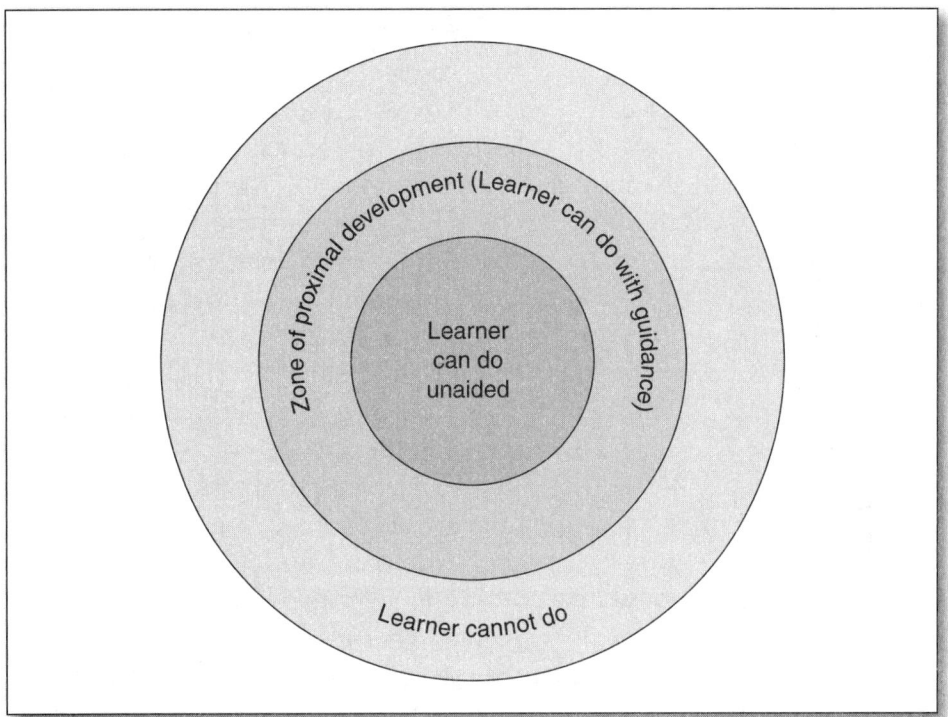

a situation where they feel as if they are being judged and deemed unsuccessful. It is also less effective for coaches to solely focus on what the teacher can do unaided. This steers coaching toward praise or conciliatory feedback. Finding the ZPD is essential for *providing strengths-based feedback*. In Lessons From the Field, you will learn how a coach did just that.

LESSONS FROM THE FIELD

Sandra has been a literacy coach at Edison Elementary School for the past six years. Before that, she was a teacher at the school. When Sandra first became a coach, she felt uncomfortable engaging in dialogue with her fellow teachers. These were her friends, people whom she had taught alongside, and suddenly she was their coach. This felt strange to her. In her first few weeks on the job, Sandra attended a professional development session for the coaches in her district.

(Continued)

(Continued)

A big take-away was a list of questions that she could use to guide her coaching conversations. This was a great starting point for Sandra because it gave her language by which she could engage with the teachers in her school. What she didn't anticipate was the fact that even with the handy set of questions, she still felt uncomfortable in her new coaching role. Her principal didn't do much to assuage this discomfort, especially when he requested that Sandra "move people with feedback." She wasn't sure how she would navigate this expectation while also staying student-centered.

Fast forward five years, and you'll find that a lot has changed for Sandra. She has found her voice as a coach and has even figured out how to provide feedback in a way that "moves people." Around the time she was developing her skill as a coach, Sandra was also earning a master's degree in second-language acquisition. She was learning about the social nature of learning, scaffolding, and the zone of proximal development. What were educational theories in the context of language acquisition seemed relevant to her coaching work as well. So she set out to find a way to blend these two seemingly different worlds.

It came together during a coaching cycle with Andy, an experienced kindergarten teacher in her school. Andy resembled a big teddy bear and was loved by both the parents and students. He had a certain charisma, and he certainly knew how to make kindergarten fun. What led Andy to a coaching cycle was his discomfort with the new expectations that were, in his words, "being foisted on kindergarten teachers." Viewing Sandra as an ally, he signed up for a coaching cycle with the goal to "Figure out how to navigate the new standards in a way that would be good for my kids." Sandra viewed this as a terrific opening and understood that there was no point in working against Andy. She would find a way to work with him.

Thinking back to what she was learning in graduate school, Sandra set out to determine Andy's ZPD. Where was the space where he would have the most potential as a learner? She decided that rather than guessing, she would include Andy in the conversation. Their first conversation is detailed in Figure 8.3.

As Sandra sat with Andy, she knew that she had to find an area that he was interested in pursuing within his goal for student learning. He was discouraged and was feeling undervalued as a teacher, and the last thing she wanted to do was add to his frustration. Yet,

Figure 8.3 Sandra and Andy's Initial Conversation

Sandra:	You've shared your frustrations with the new standards. How about if we think through what we might work on during our coaching cycle? What are you working on in literacy? Maybe we can start there?
Andy:	Sure. We are working on phonemic awareness, I've been teaching the students rhyming words, and we've been doing it with songs and poems. I'm also about to start a unit on reading informational text. I have a great collection of beautiful nonfiction books that the kids love.
Sandra:	Great, that sounds like two good options.
Andy:	But what I really need help with is making the case for play-based kindergarten. The principal doesn't seem to value what I do, and I'm not about to make my kindergartners start writing paragraphs.
Sandra:	I understand that you are frustrated. Is there an area in your teaching that excites you? Where is there potential for you to grow?
Andy:	That's a good question. I have been thinking about building more opportunities for my students to be curious and question. I love the book *A Place for Wonder* by Georgia Heard, and I'm interested in working some of her ideas into my classroom.
Sandra:	That would fit really well with your nonfiction unit. And the kindergarten standards (*refers directly to the standards*) do mention understanding and using question words. We may even be able to weave that into your work with phonemic awareness, too.
Andy:	That's good to know. I do think this is an area that I'm interested in. Let's go for it.

she also didn't want to their work to become a complaint session or praise-fest. If she was going to find his ZPD, then she had to find out what energized him.

But understanding what excited Andy was just the beginning. Sandra's next step was to implement a coaching cycle that stayed true to his focus and moved his students along. Before they got started, Sandra asked if there was anything he wanted her to be sure to do as his coach, and he said, "You know me, I always want feedback. If you are in my room, then I want to know what you are thinking." Figure 8.4 illustrates how Sandra went about delivering on this request.

(Continued)

(Continued)

Figure 8.4 Providing Strengths-Based Feedback within Andy's Coaching Cycle

Step 1: Sandra Begins by Clarifying

Sandra: Thanks for letting me participate in the lesson today. I feel like we are getting used to teaching together and the kids seem to like it, too.

Andy: I agree. It's so nice to have you in the room. I feel like we can get to a lot more kids.

Sandra: How about if we look at some of the student evidence that we collected. Our learning target was "I can use who, what, when, and where words." We took anecdotal notes in a few ways. The students were questioning at your aquarium. That was fun. They were questioning during the read aloud. And they were questioning each other during the share session. I don't know about you, but I collected a lot of data. What did you notice? And what did you wonder?

Andy: I noticed that they are getting more used to using the words. Some of my second-language learners seemed a little bit tongue-tied. Like Marco, he was interchanging the words in some interesting ways. I also think it was a good idea to wait to introduce "why." We can do that next since it's less concrete.

Sandra: Did you notice any students using the sentence starters that we introduced earlier this week?

Andy: Yes, a few even looked at the bookmark that listed them. Others seemed more stuck.

Sandra: Let's talk more about that. What were you thinking when you noticed that they were stuck?

Andy: *(Responds with more examples.)*

Step 2: Sandra Values What She Saw

Sandra: You know what is really exciting? All of your students are trying on the language in all different ways. I think that having the questioning words woven throughout the lesson, at the aquarium, in the read aloud, and through the share session gave them so much opportunity to practice. It also seems like you are staying true to your constructivist beliefs and teaching to the new standards. What do you think about that?

Andy: I guess so. I was excited to hear the buzz in the room. For a minute I just listened and I heard so many question words flying around.

Sandra: I agree.

> **Step 3: Sandra and Andy Uncover Possibilities**
>
> Sandra: So, where do we go from here?
>
> Andy: Your point about the bookmark with the sentence starters got me thinking. Only a few students are using them, and I think that it is a great scaffold. What if we modeled using the bookmark during a conversation? Maybe you and I can do that together?
>
> Sandra: Absolutely! How would you like to set that up?
>
> Andy: I have some interesting animal skulls from my science bin . . . that would get their attention. What if I put them out on a table, and you and I asked each other questions about them?
>
> Sandra: That's a great idea. Then we can add that as a wonder station. We might also want to remind them to use the sentence starters during the share session . . . they'd have to have the bookmarks handy.
>
> Andy: I agree. And I can have the sentence stems on chart paper during the read aloud.
>
> Sandra: So we'll keep the learning target the same. Any thoughts on how we'll collect student evidence?
>
> Andy: Let's do it the same way but be sure that we look for how they are using the sentence stems. I see them as a scaffold, so I don't want to make them use the stems if they don't need them. But if they are struggling, then I hope it will help.
>
> Sandra: Sounds like a great lesson.

In this conversation, Sandra accomplished two things. First, she helped Andy make the connection between what he felt was important (wondering and curiosity) with the standards that he was so unsure of. By doing so, she helped him understand that we don't have to pick one over the other.

Andy's "+1," or the thing that Sandra felt would push his teaching one step further, was encouraging the students to more actively use the sentence starters as a scaffold for their language development. In the past, Andy hadn't scaffolded language in this way, and Sandra knew that it was essential for the second language learners in his classroom.

As they continued through the cycle, the students became more and more able to engage in the kinds of conversations that Andy was looking for. Sandra continued to organize her planning sessions using the three-step process for strengths-based feedback and Andy felt

(Continued)

> (Continued)
>
> that he was finding common ground between his teaching style and the standards. As they moved toward wrapping up the cycle, Sandra wondered, "You said that you wanted feedback if I was going to be in your room. Do you feel like you got it?" He responded, "I do think I got feedback, but it wasn't the old-fashioned kind, like I get during my evaluations. It did push me, and I'm doing new things in my classroom because of it."

TOOLS AND TECHNIQUES

Troubleshooting Conversations About Feedback

Feedback can mean a lot of things to a lot of people. Some teachers cringe when they hear the word *feedback*. Others want as much as they can get. Discussing what feedback looks like in a coaching cycle is essential to the norm-setting process. The language in Figure 8.5 provides strategies for engaging in these conversations.

Figure 8.5 Language for *Providing Strengths-Based Feedback*

If I hear . . .	Then I can use the following language . . .
[Teacher says] I love feedback. The more the better. Don't mince words and just tell me where I stand.	It's great that you are such a learner and that you are so comfortable with feedback. I believe in providing strengths-based feedback. This means that we will celebrate what's going well and also think about what we can do better.
[Principal says] I'm worried about some teachers in our school. I'd like to see you using feedback to improve their instruction.	Feedback is definitely a part of my coaching, but not in an evaluative way. If I don't focus on what the teachers want to work toward, then it feels like I am judging (or fixing) them. I will definitely work with teachers on their instructional goals, but it will be in partnership. If you have serious concerns, then we might have to brainstorm some other ways to handle it.
[Teacher says] I'm worried about my latest interim assessments. Can you let me know what I can be doing better?	How about if we start by looking at how the students did (clarify and value). Then we can brainstorm what to do next (uncover possibilities).

Questions for Personal Reflection

When it comes to providing feedback, one of your best sources of insight is yourself. Think about a time when you were engaged in new learning. Were you learning to cook? Do a craft? Play a sport? Reflect on how feedback helped you improve, and apply this experience to how you work with other adult learners (see Figure 8.6).

Figure 8.6 Personal Reflection

1. Think about a time when you learned something new. Why did you choose this new learning?
2. What challenges did you face in this new learning?
3. How did feedback support your development?
4. How can you apply what you experienced to your coaching?

Using Strengths-Based Feedback During Collaborative Learning

This chapter has focused on providing feedback during one-on-one coaching conversations. But we also find that quality feedback can support collaborative learning such as data teams or professional learning communities. The protocol in Figure 8.7 provides a format for supporting small groups as they work to provide feedback to one another.

Figure 8.7 Protocol for Providing Strengths-Based Feedback in Teams

Purpose: Provide strengths-based feedback on a lesson plan, student work, or a unit of study.

1. **Presentation of Your Work (5–10 minutes)**
   The presenting teacher shares any of the following: an upcoming lesson, student data, a unit of study, a set of learning targets, or so on. Participants listen and take notes.

2. **Clarifying Questions (5 minutes)**
   Participants ask clarifying questions. Clarifying may sound like "Did I hear you say . . . ?" or "Can you tell me more about . . . ?"

(Continued)

> **Figure 8.7** (Continued)
>
> 3. **Value Statements (5 minutes)**
>   Participants make statements that highlight positive aspects of the plan. Valuing may sound like "It sounds like you have . . . " "There is a lot of evidence of . . . " or "You have developed . . . "
> 4. **Possibility Thinking (10 minutes)**
>   Participants discuss the "and," or next step, that will take the presenter further in his or her work. To do so, they build off of what's working already. Possibility thinking may sound like "Where to next?" "How can we help?" "Would it make sense to . . . ?" Comments are made in an invitational manner, therefore sending the signal that the presenting teacher maintains ownership over what happens in the classroom.

Language for Providing Strengths-Based Feedback

Developing your own language for providing feedback is an important step to feeling comfortable with this coaching move. Rather than viewing Figure 8.8 as a script, think of it as examples of how we use language to

> **Figure 8.8** Language Stems
>
> Step 1: Clarify
>
> - I noticed the students doing . . . Can you tell me more about that?
> - How did you plan for . . . ?
> - What data did you use to make that decision?
> - What steps did you take to get there?
> - Do you think . . . was because of . . . ?
>
> Step 2: Value
>
> - The students really responded to . . .
> - Look at how the students engaged in . . .
> - . . . was really effective.
> - You really thought about . . .
> - I know you've been working on . . . It's starting to take shape.
>
> Step 3: Uncover Possibilities
>
> - How can we transfer what we saw to other situations?
> - What are some possibilities for . . . ?
> - What are some ways we could . . . ?
> - We can try . . . or . . . What do you think?
> - What would it look like if we tried . . . ?

progress through the three stages of *providing strengths-based feedback*. Feel free to try this language on and develop your own.

A FINAL THOUGHT

As coaches, it's our job to learn how to provide feedback in ways that stretch learning but also honor our partnerships with teachers. We have to remember that at times, adult learners may have a crisis of confidence. Teachers often feel beat up. They may want to give up. Or they may want to hide out in their classrooms and hope that nobody notices them. These are the situations when *providing strengths-based feedback* can really make a difference in the lives of teachers because it honors them and provides the "and" that they need to learn and grow.

If we hope to see our feedback take root, then we must maintain whatever discipline is necessary to view adult learners in a positive light. We must honor them and take an asset-based perspective (much as we hope they do with their students). If we fail at this, then all of our hard work to develop respectful partnerships flies right out the window.

It is also helpful to remember that everyone is on his or her own learning progression, and good feedback is just what we need to feel motivated to keep going. This is exactly what Angela and Jeff provided to Diane on the ski slopes. They provided timely feedback that met her right where she was. When Diane ran into them a few months later, she said, "I'm ready for your next tip!" While she had had her moments, and a few crashes, she hadn't given up and was eager for more feedback. They watched her make a few turns and pointed out that she was doing a better job with her ski poles. Angela suggested that she move her bent knee back so she can get more power through her turns. She even said, "It's the natural progression, and you are ready for it." Diane is no fool; she knew that there were probably scores of tips that they could have given her. But they didn't want her to give up, so they picked the most important one. Just as Vygotsky would have suggested.

9 Measuring the Impact of Coaching

In the 1989 Hollywood classic *Field of Dreams*, the main character Ray, played by Kevin Costner, is walking through his Iowa cornfield one summer evening. Suddenly, he hears a mysterious voice say, "If you build it, they will come." Understandably perplexed, Ray sets out on a mission to figure out the meaning of this cryptic message. He comes to find out that it is in reference to a baseball field, which he ultimately decides to build smack dab in the middle of all that corn even though he risks losing the entire farm to do it. Not surprisingly, everyone thinks he has lost his mind by taking such a huge leap of faith. Thankfully, that prophetic statement, bellowed in the legendary voice of James Earl Jones, proves to be true. The final scene of the movie shows a long line of cars traveling down a stretch of road on a warm summer night. They've come to watch the magical games of baseball that are being played on Ray's field of dreams.

For much of our careers as instructional coaches, we have operated under a similar principle. But ours was more like "If you do it, they will learn." *You* referred to the teachers we were coaching. *It* was the practice or curriculum we were tasked with getting them to implement. And *they* were the students. The thinking was that if we could just coach teachers to *do* something—be it a practice, structure, program, or curriculum—then student achievement would increase. Yet, after many years of coaching based on this premise, and after hearing from countless coaches from across the country, it has become clear that it is not enough to simply trust that doing *something* would yield results. As coaches we need to *know* how we are impacting learning. *Measuring the impact* is a coaching move that lets us do just that. It enables us to make decisions not on assumptions or leaps of faith like Ray but rather on actual evidence of student performance, teacher growth, feedback, and personal reflection.

THE MOVE—*MEASURING THE IMPACT OF COACHING*

Throughout this book, we have talked about ways that we collect evidence of student learning, such as through pre-assessments at the beginning of a coaching cycle, when co-teaching in the classroom, and when sorting student work after a lesson. So, in effect, you could say that we are measuring the impact of our coaching every step of the way. But when we talk about the coaching move *measuring the impact of coaching*, we are referring specifically to the collection of steps we take at the end of a coaching cycle to figure out how it went—for the students, teacher, and coach.

Figure 9.1 reminds us of how we progress through a coaching cycle. At the beginning, we partner with teachers to create a goal for student learning. During our planning conversations, we analyze student evidence to design instruction. As we reach the end of the coaching cycle, we look carefully at the impact of our work in order to create space for closure. We want to know if students met the goal that was set at the beginning of the cycle, and we want to take time for the teacher and coach to reflect on what they learned throughout the process.

WHY *MEASURING THE IMPACT OF COACHING* IS IMPORTANT

When Diane and Leanna started working as staff developers, the notion of job-embedded professional development was brand new. Today, school districts across the country are investing substantial amounts of money and other resources into instructional coaches. Naturally, they want to know if their investment is paying off. As Diane (Sweeney, 2013) explains in *Student-Centered Coaching*, "Educators are clamoring for a way to collect evaluation data that proves how coaching positively impacts students, yet a large group of researchers believe we can only indirectly measure the impact of coaching on student learning. Couple this with the times in which we find ourselves—with increasing pressure to demonstrate the efficacy of every penny we are spending in our schools—and it becomes clear that we can't settle for measuring only indirectly whether coaching

Figure 9.1 Stages in a Coaching Cycle

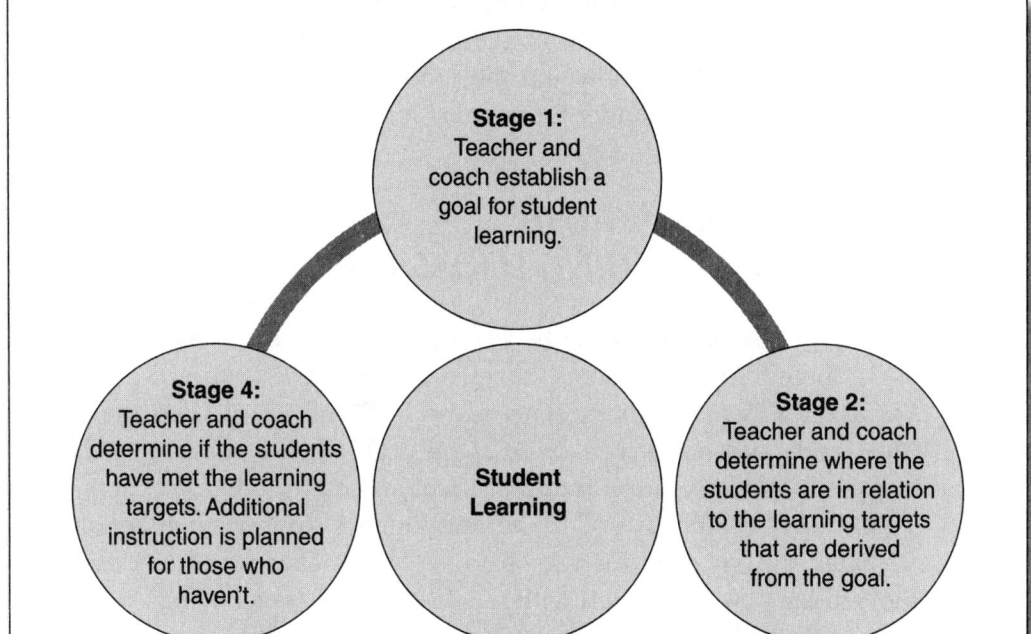

has made an impact. We have to know for sure" (p. 85). In order to know whether or not what we're doing is having the desired effect, we need a process to gather and interpret information about the work of students, teachers, and coaches.

The first thing we can do to measure our impact is to look directly at student work. We need to know if students have met the learning goal that was set at the beginning of the coaching cycle. It is also important for teachers to know if engaging in a coaching cycle was an effective use of their time and for coaches to know if there was a lasting impact on instruction. We do this is by evaluating our work in a way that is not only results-focused, but process-focused as well (Killion, 2008).

In Chapter 6, we learned about the value of being metacognitive. John Dewey also reminds us that "we do not learn from experience . . . we learn from *reflecting* on experience." Reflecting on all that took place throughout a coaching cycle, coupled with evidence of student achievement, gives us feedback on both the results and the process itself. *Measuring the impact of coaching* provides rich fodder for ongoing learning and professional growth.

WHAT *MEASURING THE IMPACT OF COACHING* LOOKS LIKE

A group of coaches was recently asked, "How do you measure your success?" Some common answers that emerged in the discussion were "When I get asked to work with a teacher again," "When people seek me out for help," and "When teachers smile at me." One brave coach added, with plenty of self-deprecating humor, "I feel successful when teachers don't avoid me in the hallway and in the staff lounge!" Indeed, many of us have evaluated our success this way because in the absence of any evidence from students, we aren't left with much else upon which to base our effectiveness. Yet, when we take intentional steps to evaluate our work, it provides both teachers and coaches with insights to inform their practice moving forward.

QR Code 9.1
Reflecting on the Coaching Cycle With a Third-Grade Team

http://qrs.ly/lb59nvg

Pre- and Post-Assess to Identify Growth Across a Coaching Cycle

If coaches really want to know the impact of their work with teachers, then they need to collect pre- and post-assessment data during the coaching cycle. In Chapter 2, we discussed the importance of having clearly defined learning targets against which we continually assess and adjust teaching. This starts with pre-assessing students to collect baseline data at the beginning of the coaching cycle. Then at the end of the cycle, we post-assess students in order to measure student growth and understand the impact of the coaching work.

The assessments we use have several qualities in order to be both manageable and meaningful for teachers and coaches. They are efficient, provide descriptive insight into student thinking and understanding, and are aligned with the learning targets and goal for students. When we post-assess to see whether or not students have met the goal, it is important to make sure we are assessing the same things as we did on the pre-assessment. Figure 9.2 gives some

Figure 9.2 Modifications From Pre- to Post-Assessment

Pre-Assessment	Post-Assessment
Read a passage, annotate text, and answer questions with evidence from the text.	Use a slightly different passage from the same text. Keep everything else the same.
Complete a multistep math problem with multiple opportunities to show work. Explain thinking in writing.	Use the same problem, just switch the numbers.
Write to a prompt that is open ended enough for some amount of student choice.	Keep the prompt the same, instructing students to choose something different to write about.
Written response to a series of open-ended questions about historical events.	Respond to the same questions in a new way, such as through a Socratic Seminar.

examples of how a pre-assessment can be modified to also serve as a post-assessment. Keeping them as similar as possible will give the most accurate measurement of student growth.

Once we have post-assessed the students, we can take a good look at growth. This can be the percentage of students who met the goal or a more nuanced view of how many were emerging, developing, meeting, or exceeding the goal at the beginning of the coaching cycle compared to at the end. Seeing real evidence of student achievement is a great way to *measure the impact of coaching* and know that the hard work of teaching and coaching has paid off.

Plan for Students Who Didn't Meet the Goal

The past fifteen years have seen a switch in education from *covering* curriculum to teaching in a way that enables and expects all students to meet the standards. The notion of "assess and move on, regardless of whether or not students got it" is thankfully becoming a thing of the past. This shift has implications for coaches just as it does for the teachers with whom they work. With a clear goal for student learning and carefully planned instruction based on ongoing formative assessment, students are given the support and tools they need to achieve the desired learning outcome. But sometimes despite our best efforts, there are a few kids who don't get there.

Measuring the impact of coaching through post-assessment enables the coach and teacher to identify those students (hopefully very few) who did not meet the goal and then plan for ongoing support even after the coaching cycle is over. Sometimes the school may have a more formal Response to Intervention (RTI) system in place, or it may be a matter of the teacher and coach creating a plan for how the teacher will use small group or one-on-one instructional time to give the extra help needed. Even though the coaching cycle is over and the class is going to move on to something new, it is important to identify and plan follow-up for those students who still need a bit more instruction before they can meet the goal. We are also careful to set up systems to continue monitoring these students through formative assessments—this way we make sure that they are moving toward mastery of the standards well past the end of the coaching cycle.

Facilitate Teacher Reflection

A common theme throughout this book has been how our coaching has grown and changed as a result of becoming more student-centered in our approach. As we have moved away from implicitly trying to fix teachers, we have experienced far more buy-in and have been able to document tremendous student growth. But by placing the focus on student achievement, we do not mean to imply that teacher growth has been thrown out the window. Rather, while the primary goal of coaching is student learning, we are continually working toward teacher capacity building as an additional outcome of the coaching experience. If a coach and teacher work together throughout a coaching cycle, and the students demonstrate a lot of growth by the end, surely that is cause for celebration. Hopefully the kids have learned new skills and understandings that they will carry forward in their learning and be able to apply in new situations. Yet, consider how much bigger an impact the coaching will have if the *teacher* has acquired new learning as well. The benefit will be not only to this one group of students for this one unit of study but for all of the students throughout the teacher's career. Now that is a big impact!

So how do we assess teacher growth as a part of *measuring the impact of coaching*? We know that our job is to stay as far away from evaluation as possible. We also know that reflection on experience is a powerful way to enhance and solidify learning. Therefore, at the end of a cycle, it is important to create opportunities for the teacher to reflect on the coaching experience. There are many informal opportunities to encourage teacher reflection throughout the coaching cycle by asking questions such as "How do you think the lesson went?" "How did students respond compared to when you taught this in the past?" and "What could we have done differently to help more students meet the target?" When *measuring the impact of coaching*, we want to explicitly make time for reflection through asking a series of exit interview questions that we can document as evidence of teacher growth. Though some coaches feel that conducting such an interview seems awkwardly formal, we believe that intentionally doing so creates both a space for reflection and an opportunity to capture evidence that comes directly from teachers themselves instead from us as their coaches. A few examples of exit interview questions aimed at promoting teacher reflection are included in Figure 9.3.

Figure 9.3 Exit Interview Questions for Teacher Reflection

- How do you feel you benefited from the coaching cycle?
- What changes, if any, have you made to your instructional practice as a result of our work together?
- What does the student evidence reveal about how the students performed in relation to the learning targets?
- What about the way we taught the unit do you believe contributed to this result?
- What, if anything, do you feel we could have done differently with regard to instruction?
- How has your thinking grown or changed from this process?
- Based on the work in our coaching cycle, what are the implications for your work going forward?

Think About Ongoing Support

When Keri was in her second year as a high school coach, she had built great relationships with much of the staff and was really starting to see the impact of her coaching cycles. She loved working closely with teachers and their students. Where she struggled was bringing her coaching cycles to an end. Sometimes the teacher got so comfortable with their partnership that she feared she'd created a sense of dependency. Other times they were just in a great groove, and she felt they still had so much they could work on together.

Many of us experience these same concerns as we wind up our coaching cycles. We wonder, "How can we end a cycle and yet still continue to provide assistance to the teachers we have worked with?" But just as we create openings for coaching, we must create closings as well. Sometimes this takes place when we help a teacher plan for the students who didn't meet the goal, as we discussed earlier in this chapter. Or maybe the teacher and coach decide to schedule a time to touch base once a week over several weeks so the coach can continue to help with the students—albeit more from a distance now. Or it can look like a "well care" checkup that we would schedule with a doctor; a set time once a month or so when we just check in to make sure everything is going okay. Other times we may see themes from our coaching work that can turn into small group or whole school professional development. This could take the form of a book study, shared learning on a teacher release day, or setting up opportunities for facilitated classroom observations around a common focus. Whichever form it takes, what matters is that we use the information we get at the end of coaching cycles to guide us in providing meaningful ongoing support to the teachers we have collaborated with.

Solicit Feedback and Self-Reflect

Leanna was recently working with a team of coaches who had been implementing student-centered coaching in their district for over a year. At the end of a full day of shared learning, they had time to pose some of their lingering questions to discuss with one another. A coach raised her hand and asked, "What do you do if after a whole coaching cycle, you go into a teacher's room a few weeks later and see that everything has gone back to the way it was before?" A few of the other coaches chimed in with stories of similar experiences. "In Mr. H's class, I spent weeks getting him set up with math centers and then found out later that he wasn't even doing them anymore," said one coach. Then another shared, "We had the kids giving each other such amazing feedback on their projects in biology class, but now the teacher told me it doesn't work as well without me there in the room."

The question, along with the stories that followed, raised some red flags for Leanna, but she wanted to be sure to put it back on the coaches. "Okay," she started, "when you were still a teacher and you taught a lesson and got a totally different outcome from what you expected, what did you do?" Hands shot up without hesitation. "Asked myself what I could have done differently," said one. "Talked with the kids to find out what wasn't clear," offered another. "I would look at their assignments and try to find where the breakdown was and then think about what I needed to do in another way," explained a third coach. Several people nodded in agreement. Leanna let everyone sit with this for a moment before posing a question back to the group. "As teachers, we solicit feedback and we self-reflect. So, what does this mean for us as coaches?"

If we are working from a partnership approach in coaching, we cannot make the analogy that the teachers we work with are just like our students. They are our colleagues, and it is not our job to fix them. Yet, just as we understand the value of using feedback and reflection to improve our instruction as teachers, we can also use these tools to help us continually grow in our practice as coaches. So instead of wondering what to *do* about a certain teacher who hasn't responded the way we would have hoped, we should consider soliciting feedback from them about what did and didn't go well in the coaching cycle and ask ourselves the same thing. But this is not just for when things didn't go as planned. Reflection is a powerful tool for learning, and we can make feedback and self-reflection an integrated part of *measuring the impact of coaching* at the end of each and every coaching cycle. Later in this chapter you will meet Jen, and you will see how she did just that as part of an exit interview with a teacher named Darcy.

Celebrate!

In today's educational climate, the very word *evaluate* has become fraught with negativity. Too often we experience evaluation in education to focus solely on what we're doing wrong, what our kids don't know, and where our kids aren't showing enough growth. Rarely do we take time to focus on what *is* working and what we are doing *right*. But if we want to create a culture where coaching is for everybody and it's not about fixing teachers, we need to put the emphasis on the positive and celebrate the results of our coaching efforts.

QR Code 9.2
Reflecting at the End of a Coaching Cycle, Sixth-Grade Math

http://qrs.ly/ i459nvr

There are many ways to share the great work that happens when teachers and coaches get together to collaborate deeply around student achievement. Principals often do this by sharing student growth that has been shown from a pre- to post-assessment—through their weekly email to teachers, at a staff meeting, or when speaking with fellow administrators. Coaches can do the same both through their formal and informal modes of communication. Equally powerful is to hear teachers' own reflections on the coaching experience. When given the chance to share the changes they have seen in their students and the how their practice has grown, it sends an important message about the value of coaching. When we *measure the impact of coaching* we create opportunities to celebrate the successes of students, teachers, and coaches.

LESSONS FROM THE FIELD

Jen and Darcy were sitting in Jen's cozy office huddled in front of a post-assessment that they had just been analyzing. "Wow," exclaimed Jen, "when we first started only one student kind of got it, and now all but three are totally there!" The duo just spent the past five weeks in a coaching cycle focused on getting Darcy's fourth-grade students to use text clues and background knowledge to infer and increase comprehension when reading in science. Jen recorded the post-assessment data and found that 88% of students met or exceeded the goal. She asked Darcy, "So what's the plan for these three kiddos that still aren't there yet?" Darcy suggested going back to some easier texts unrelated to the content to get them to slow down and listen to their thinking, which she could do while pulling them as a small group during independent work time. Jen recorded this on the front page of the Results-Based Coaching Tool that she had pulled up on her laptop (Figure 9.4).

Feeling confident that there was a plan for follow-up, Jen launched into her exit interview questions. "We know that your kids showed huge growth, but can you tell me more about the impact our work had on them? What else are you seeing?" Darcy didn't hesitate in sharing that her kids are much more engaged in science class and in reading in general. They are being much more metacognitive and recognizing other strategies in addition to inferring. And they are working much more independently during workshop time.

"What about you? How do you feel you benefited from our collaboration during this coaching cycle?" Jen asked. Darcy drew in a deep breath and slowly let it out: "This process made me so much more reflective. Taking the time to look at student work with you and to sort it into piles . . . it gave me such a clear focus on where they are. It made my mini lessons and even my conferences more powerful. And I use my time so much better now because I know how to prioritize what matters instructionally. I feel like I use every minute so intentionally, which I didn't always do before." She paused before continuing: "Teaching this long block in the afternoon used to be tough. But it's amazing to see how much more engaged the kids are now with all the changes we've made and how much more they're learning." Jen nodded in agreement while busily typing up everything Darcy was saying.

"Let's talk more specifically about the coaching itself. What was most beneficial out of everything we did together?" Jen asked. "Everything, really," Darcy said with a laugh. "Looking at student work, like I said, but also thinking through the mini-lessons together, having you help me build up a workshop for science, talking about which texts to use . . . even when you would just jump in and say things differently to the kids. Honestly, I really got so much out of working together with you!" Clearly the coaching cycle was a positive experience for both Darcy and her students, but Jen didn't want to stop there. "I'm glad that you got so much out of this. I learned a lot, too. What about any challenges or missed opportunities?" They sat in silence for a minute before Darcy spoke. "I think the hardest thing was time. We would just get into the meat of something and then get interrupted. I always wanted more time to plan and think things through together." Jen agreed, though she didn't really have any solutions to offer. "I also think it was hard to start with such a big concept like inferring," Darcy continued. "I think we could have started with more accessible text and focusing just on text clues for a while and then on activating background knowledge. I guess it worked okay because we backed up and did it anyway when we saw they weren't getting it, but it would have been better to start there." Jen agreed. She also shared that as a coach she felt she could have done a better job of keeping them on track toward the end of the cycle when things started to drag on. They both laughed. "Yeah, but we still got there in the end," Darcy said. And it was true. Even while acknowledging some things that could have gone differently, Darcy and Jen were able to celebrate tremendous growth for the students and for themselves. They spent a few more minutes talking about some ways that Jen could continue to support Darcy even though they would no longer be in a coaching cycle together, and they wrapped up the meeting with a big hug.

After Darcy headed out to pick up her fourth graders from music class, Jen sat in her office for a minute to take it all in. She read over what she had captured from their conversation, then did some further reflecting on her own coaching on the second page of the Results-Based Coaching Tool (Figure 9.4). Jen agreed that she and

(Continued)

> (Continued)
>
> Darcy worked really well together. She had wanted to focus on asking more reflective questions during their planning times and felt this helped her from doing too much of the talking. She also agreed that issues with scheduling got in the way of their coaching at times and made a note to bring this up with the principal at their next meeting. Thinking specifically about her coaching practice, Jen thought she could have been more effective when co-teaching in Darcy's classroom. With these things in mind, Jen resolved to do a little more learning around co-teaching and to keep focusing on reflective questions in her coaching conversations moving forward. All in all, Jen felt very positive about how this coaching cycle went. Measuring and documenting student growth from pre- to post-assessment was an important part of understanding the effect of her collaboration with Darcy. But taking the time for feedback and reflection also proved to be an invaluable resource in *measuring the impact* of Jen's coaching.

TOOLS AND TECHNIQUES

Results-Based Coaching Tool

The Results-Based Coaching Tool (Figure 9.4) is a place to document and tell the story of a coaching cycle. On the first page, it starts with the goal for students and ends with the results of how students did toward meeting that goal, including follow-up for those who didn't quite make it. In between is where we capture instructional practices, coaching practices, and teacher growth.

A team of coaches in Clark County, Nevada came up with the brilliant idea of adding a place on the Results-Based Coaching Tool to document reflections of both the teacher and the coach, as shown in Figure 9.5 (see page 147).

Figure 9.4 Jen and Darcy's Results-Based Coaching Tool

Teacher: Darcy			Coach: Jen	
Coaching Cycle Focus: Inferring in fourth-grade science and using the workshop model.			**Dates of Coaching Cycle:** 10/16/2015–11/26/2015	
Standards-Based Goal What is the goal for student learning?	**Focus for Teacher Learning** What instructional practices will help students reach the goal?	**Student-Centered Coaching** What coaching practices were implemented during this coaching cycle?	**Teacher Learning** As a result of the coaching cycle, what instructional practices are being used on a consistent basis?	**Student Learning** How did student achievement increase as a result of the coaching cycle?
Students will . . . Refer to text clues and background knowledge when explaining what the text says and when drawing inferences. *Standard(s):* RI.4.1 and RL.4.1 *Learning Targets:* I can • Annotate my thinking in the text • Record facts to remember what is important • Use text features to learn more information	Teacher will . . . Model the following: • Model annotating text, identifying important information, and activating background knowledge • Instruct whole group, small group, and individually, using a workshop structure • Construct and use anchor charts • Post and unpack learning targets with students	Coach and Teacher did . . . (check those that apply) ☐ Goal setting ☐ Creating learning targets ☐ Analysis of student work ☐ Co-teaching ☐ Collecting student evidence during the class period ☐ Collaborative planning ☐ Shared learning to build knowledge of content and pedagogy	Teacher is . . . • Consistently using the workshop model across content areas • Implementing and realizing the power of a quick, explicit mini-lesson • Offering student choice within the workshop model, which eliminates most behavior problems	Students are . . . • Working more independently • Using a variety of comprehension strategies • More engaged in reading *Post-Assessment Data:* 0-Emerging 3-Developing 20-Meeting 2-Exceeding

(Continued)

145

Figure 9.4 (Continued)

Teacher: Darcy	Coach: Jen		
• Identify important details in a text • Activate my background knowledge when reading • Use my background knowledge and text clues to infer *Baseline Data:* 24-Emerging 1-Developing 0-Meeting 0-Exceeding 1/25 Students were able to infer using text clues and background knowledge when reading a designated text.			22/25 students were able to infer using text clues and background knowledge when reading a designated text. *Follow-up for students who didn't reach the goal:* • Look at holes in their learning . . . more time recognizing and building background knowledge • Spend more time building vocabulary in order to connect to a piece of text • Work on determining important information within a text • Practice with easier text not in content area

Figure 9.5 Reflection Questions for the Results-Based Coaching Tool

Teacher Reflections	Coach Reflections
What worked well for you during our collaboration and coaching cycle? How was your teaching been positively impacted?	What worked well for you during our collaboration and coaching cycle?
How do you feel our collaboration has positively impacted the students?	How do you feel our collaboration positively impacted the students?
What were any challenges or missed opportunities during our work together?	What were any challenges or missed opportunities during our work together?
What are some next steps in your teaching?	What are some next steps in my coaching?

Troubleshooting Around Measuring the Impact of Coaching

Bringing the coaching cycle to a close and taking the time to intentionally think about the effect of our work is an important component of student-centered coaching. The if/then chart shown in Figure 9.6 addresses some of the obstacles that might be found with this coaching move.

Figure 9.6 Language for Measuring the Impact of Coaching

If I'm thinking or finding . . .	Then I should remember that . . .
Teachers feel overwhelmed by the thought of having to do more pre- and post-assessments.	The data we collect to evaluate the impact of coaching should be easy to create and efficient to analyze. If we're clear about what we want to know and how we're asking it, this will be a valuable tool that doesn't require a lot of extra time and work.
I'm worried that the Results-Based Coaching Tool will be used for my formal evaluation as a coach, and I've heard teachers expressing the same concern.	The purpose of the Results-Based Coaching Tool is to keep our work focused, to create opportunities for reflection, and above all for celebration. It is not intended to rate or judge teachers or coaches.
I have a really comfortable relationship with this teacher, and so doing an actual exit interview seems too formal and awkward. He's already told me how much he's learned, and I know how well the kids did, too.	Taking the time to intentionally reflect is key to learning. And documenting is a great way to celebrate growth. If it doesn't feel comfortable asking the reflection questions aloud, they can always be completed in writing.

A FINAL THOUGHT

Ray took a huge leap of faith in building a baseball field right in the middle of his crop of corn, and it paid off. No doubt some of our coaching has an impact on student achievement, even when we don't have much evidence to tell us so. But think about how much more effective our coaching becomes when we *know* what's working instead of just making assumptions. *Measuring the impact of coaching* provides us with multiple pieces of evidence to weigh and balance in determining what is and isn't working so we can continually improve our coaching practice. It allows us to know that our collaboration with teachers has made a difference for them and for their students. *Measuring the impact of coaching* creates a space for reflection and for closure of the coaching cycle and perhaps best of all provides us with lots of great new learning to celebrate.

In Closing

We are willing to bet that as you've been reading this book, you have been thinking a lot about your own coaching work and how these coaching moves will fit into that context. If this is the case, we are thrilled because it has been our goal to create a mental picture of what student-centered coaching looks like in action. We also hope that the video clips have supported you to further hone your understanding of the coaching moves that have filled the pages of this book.

Knowing that, your first instinct may be to try to use these coaching moves *perfectly*. This is no surprise because as educators, we hold ourselves to a very high standard. We are shaping lives after all. But when coaches ask, "Am I doing it correctly?" we struggle because when it comes to coaching, there really isn't one way to do things. Every coaching conversation is unique, with factors like relationship, teacher knowledge, and student needs influencing so much of what we do. We can't boil it down to a simple recipe that works every time. If we did, it would never work. If you are feeling this way, our advice is to be thoughtful about how you engage in this work. Make all of the tools you've read about your own. Adjust the moves to fit your situation. And trust yourself.

You may also be tempted to try to implement every one of these coaching moves right away. But we'd suggest that rather than going at it full bore, it may be more effective to take your time and base your implementation on a solid set of beliefs about your coaching practice. If you didn't get around to writing your beliefs as you read the introduction, we encourage you to do so now. They will be your beacon as you work to implement the coaching moves that you have read about in this book.

In the book *The Teacher You Want to Be,* Matt Glover and Ellin Keene (2015) write, "Unfortunately, for many of us, once we're in our classrooms, we find that our heartfelt beliefs are reduced to silent and sporadic fantasies—nice to think about on occasion, but unlikely to come true" (p. xvii). This is too often true for coaches as well. Let's put our beliefs front and center. Then let's use these coaching moves to make them a reality.

Appendix

RESOURCE A—IF/THEN CHARTS

If/Then for Goal-Setting Conversations

If I hear . . .	Then I can use the following language . . .
My students can't do anything.	What is your next unit of study? Let's take a look at the standards, and then we can figure out how to scaffold for them as learners.
I'm supposed to be using effective questioning techniques. It's on my evaluation.	That's great. We can tackle that during our coaching cycle. But let's first set a goal for your students.
I really just want you to lend me a hand. My class is out of control.	I will definitely lend you a hand when I'm in your room, but our work should focus on a goal for students. What's coming up next in your curriculum?

If/Then for Using Learning Targets

If I hear . . .	Then I can use the following language . . .
I know I'm supposed to teach to the standards, but I can't see how my kids will be able to do all that.	Let's take a look at the standards that we're going for and break them down to a set of clear learning targets. This will be our road map to get your students from where they are now to where we want them to be.
I have so much content to cover in this unit. I just don't know that I have time for learning targets, too.	I understand that there is a lot of content your students need to know. Let's also think about the type of thinking we want them to be doing around the content and create a set of targets that addresses both components of their learning.
Our district already has learning targets. Can't we just use those?	Let's use the targets we already have as a starting point. It's helpful to review what's there and decide if they align with what we are trying to accomplish. We may even unpack them further or add in something that's missing. They will guide us throughout the coaching cycle, so we want to be sure they are just right.

If/Then for Getting Ready for Coaching in the Classroom

If I hear . . .	Then I can use the following language . . .
I'd love to see you teach. Would you model it for me?	I'd be happy to model a portion of the lesson, but it may be more beneficial for us to both take part in the lesson. Let's figure out what you'd like to do and what you'd like me to do. That way we can work together.
It sounds like this might take a lot of time, especially the planning piece.	We do have to be on the same page regarding the lesson. But if we have clear learning targets, and a rough idea of what you'd like the lesson to look like, then we should be in good shape.
Are you going to observe the lesson? I really like your feedback.	We can definitely build in some observation. But it would be nice if we could work side by side during the lesson. That way, we can address anything that comes up in the moment, rather than waiting to talk about it a few days later.

If/Then for *Noticing and Naming*

If I hear . . .	Then I can use the following language . . .
I'm worried that it may be distracting to my students if you interject during the lesson.	We will be discrete about how and when we share. When we plan, you can let me know what feels best. And it's actually good for students to know where they are in relation to the learning targets.
Will it make the students feel bad?	We will make sure that we focus on the positive as well as what would stretch the students further. You can expect something like this: "Miguel is doing a great job using evidence in his summary. It looks like he is still working on his sequencing."
Will this take any more work?	I don't think so. We already have our weekly planning meeting set up so we are in good shape. And *noticing and naming* during the lesson just means that we are looking for the same things and taking notes that we can look at later.

If/Then for Micro Modeling

If I hear . . .	Then I can use the following language . . .
Can you model another lesson? You are such a great math teacher, and I don't feel like I know what I'm doing.	I'd be more than happy to *micro model* a certain part of the lesson. Which part would you feel would be most beneficial to have modeled?
[A principal says] I'd like you to show our teachers what it looks like. It is a new program and they need help getting started.	We can provide a few opportunities for teachers to observe what it looks like. But then I'd like to start helping them implement on their own. This will involve some targeted *micro modeling* but probably not a whole lesson because I'd like to create ownership that builds their capacity.
I'm not really interested in coaching. I've observed plenty of lessons, and I know what I'm doing.	I understand. I don't do a lot of modeling, but when I do, it is something specific that you ask for. Otherwise, we work as partners while in your classroom.

If/Then for Thinking Aloud

If I'm thinking or finding . . .	Then I should remember that . . .
I'm working with a brand new teacher, and it seems like it would be helpful for me to just tell him or her what to do sometimes.	Most people don't learn by you doing the thinking and making the decisions for them. When I share my thinking aloud, I am modeling how to teach and giving him or her something to reflect on.
The teacher I'm working with worries that when I share my thinking aloud to her the students think we're talking about them.	It's actually beneficial to students to know what the teacher and I are doing when we talk together in quiet voices during class time. Being metacognitive is a practice that we want all students to be engaged in, so in *thinking aloud* with a teacher we are providing them with an excellent model.
I don't even know if the thinking I'm sharing with the teacher makes sense or is what's best for the students!	As with any coaching move, this is not about being the expert or having all the right answers. Rather, the emphasis is on collaboration and modeling the importance of being reflective and thoughtful in my teaching practice.

If/Then for Sorting Student Work

If I hear . . .	Then I can use the following language . . .
I don't have time to create and grade a new test every other day to see how my kids are doing.	We want to collect student evidence that is authentic and easy to analyze. Why don't we start by taking a look at the work they've done in class today and see what we can learn from it?
I know my students really well and don't need to gather any specific evidence to know what they need.	I can tell how hard you work to know each one of your students. But if we collect actual evidence—even if it's anecdotal—we can look through it together to find trends and needs that we might not otherwise be able to catch.
It feels like a waste of my time to look through another teacher's student work. I'm not sure how that would help me and my students.	Having multiple sets of eyes on the same set of student work really creates some rich learning opportunities for everyone and helps us calibrate our understandings and expectations as a team of what success looks like and how to meet students' needs. Usually what you find in your teammates class will apply directly to your own students as well, so you won't need to go through the whole process again.

If/Then for Providing Strengths-Based Feedback

If I hear . . .	Then I can use the following language . . .
[Teacher says] I love feedback. The more the better. Don't mince words, and just tell me where I stand.	It's great that you are such a learner, and that you are so comfortable with feedback. I believe in providing strengths-based feedback. This means that we will celebrate what's going well and also think about what we can do better.
[Principal says] I'm worried about some teachers in our school. I'd like to see you using feedback to improve their instruction.	Feedback is definitely a part of my coaching, but not in an evaluative way. If I don't focus on what the teachers want to work toward, then it feels like I am judging (or fixing) them. I will definitely work with teachers on their instructional goals, but it will be in partnership. If you have serious concerns, then we might have to brainstorm some other ways to handle it.
[Teacher says] I'm worried about my latest interims. Can you let me know what I can be doing better?	How about if we start by looking at how the students did (clarify and value). Then we can brainstorm what to do next (uncover possibilities).

If/Then for Measuring the Impact of Coaching

If I'm thinking or finding . . .	Then I should remember that . . .
Teachers feel overwhelmed by the thought of having to do more pre- and post-assessments.	The data we collect to evaluate the impact of coaching should be easy to create and efficient to analyze. If we're clear about what we want to know and how we're asking it, this will be a valuable tool that doesn't require a lot of extra time and work.
I'm worried that the Results-Based Coaching Tool will be used for my formal evaluation as a coach, and I've heard teachers expressing the same concern.	The purpose of the Results-Based Coaching Tool is to keep our work focused, to create opportunities for reflection, and above all for celebration. It is not intended to rate or judge teachers or coaches.
I have a really comfortable relationship with this teacher, and so doing an actual exit interview seems too formal and awkward. He's already told me how much he's learned, and I know how well the kids did, too.	Taking the time to intentionally reflect is key to learning. And documenting is a great way to celebrate growth. If it doesn't feel comfortable asking the reflection questions aloud, they can always be completed in writing.

RESOURCE B—COACHING LOGS

Coaching Log for Noticing and Naming

Learning Target:

Student Name:	Student Name:	Student Name:	Student Name:	Student Name:
Student Name:	Student Name:	Student Name:	Student Name:	Student Name:
Student Name:	Student Name:	Student Name:	Student Name:	Student Name:
Student Name:	Student Name:	Student Name:	Student Name:	Student Name:
Student Name:	Student Name:	Student Name:	Student Name:	Student Name:

Log for Collecting Conference Notes

Learning Targets:	
Student Name:	Student Name:
Student Name:	Student Name:
Student Name:	Student Name:

Coaching Log for Noticing and Naming—Doing, Saying, and Writing

Learning Targets:
I observed students doing:
I heard students saying:
I saw students writing:

RESOURCE C—LANGUAGE STEMS

Language Stems for Goal Setting

- What do you hope the students will learn as a result of our partnership?
- Let's look at the standards. How might they help us choose a focus?
- What would you like to see your students doing as (readers, writers, mathematicians, scientists, etc.)?
- Is there any student work or data that could help us decide on a focus that would make the most impact on your students?
- How do you feel about the goal we've selected? Does it feel right to you?

Language Stems for Unpacking Standards

- What do we want the students to know and be able to do?
- What do we want the students to understand?
- What do we mean when we say the students will understand . . . ?
- How might the students demonstrate understanding?
- How can we be sure that we are thinking beyond lessons and activities?
- If we are unsure, it can be helpful to refer to the standard.
- Can you tell us more about what you are thinking?

Language Stems for Co-Planning

- What is the learning target for the lesson?
- How do we think the students will demonstrate their learning (in writing, verbally)?
- How will new content be delivered and by who?
- How will we formatively assess students?
- What resources, materials, or technology will we need to get ready?
- How will we work together to manage student behavior?

Language Stems for Micro Modeling

Questions to Ask Before *Micro Modeling*

1. What have you tried already? How did it go?
2. What impact has this had on your students?
3. Where are you feeling more or less comfortable? Why?

Questions to Ask After *Micro Modeling*

1. What did you notice about your students and their learning during the *micro modeling*?
2. What are some ways we may extend the student learning even further?
3. How did you see the students' thinking being scaffolded through dialogue and discussion?
4. How were the needs of different learners addressed (special education, English language learners, advanced learners)?

Language Stems for Thinking Aloud

- Right now I'm thinking it would make sense to . . .
- I noticed . . . so I think we should . . .
- I think we might want to . . .
- I'm wondering about . . .
- Maybe we should consider . . .
- When I see . . . it makes me think . . .

Language Stems for Providing Strengths-Based Feedback

Step 1: Clarify

- I noticed the students doing . . . Can you tell me more about that?
- How did you plan for . . .
- What data did you use to make that decision?
- What steps did you take to get there?
- Do you think . . . was because of . . . ?

Step 2: Value

- The students really responded to . . .
- Look at how the students engaged in . . .
- ___ was really effective
- You really thought about . . .
- I know you've been working on . . . It's starting to take shape.

Step 3: Uncover Possibilities

- How can we transfer what we saw to other situations?
- What are some possibilities for . . .
- What are some ways we could . . . ?

- We can try . . . or . . . What do you think?
- What would it look like if we tried . . . ?

Language Stems for Exit Interviews

- How do you feel you benefited from the coaching cycle?
- What changes, if any, have you made to your instructional practice as a result of our work together?
- What does the student evidence reveal about how the students performed in relation to the learning targets?
- What about the way we taught the unit do you believe contributed to this result?
- What, if anything, do you feel we could have done differently with regard to instruction?
- How has your thinking grown or changed from this process?
- Based on the work in our coaching cycle, what are the implications for my work going forward?

Appendix • 161

RESOURCE D—PLANNING TOOLS

Co-Planning With Learning Targets

Learning Target for Today's Lesson:		
	Plan for the Lesson	How We Will Formatively Assess
Mini Lesson:		
Work Time:		
Share Session:		

Planner for Sharing Lessons

Learning Target:

What's Happening	What It Will Look Like	Who Will Take the Lead? What Will the Other "Teacher" Do?

Four Square Planner

Whole Group Instruction:	
Focus of Instruction: Students:	Focus of Instruction: Students:
Focus of Instruction: Students:	Focus of Instruction: Students:

RESOURCE E—AGREEMENTS AND PROTOCOLS

Partnership Agreement for a Coaching Cycle

I. What Is Our Focus?

- What is our goal for student learning?
- What are the learning targets that capture what we want the students to know and be able to do?

II. How Will We Work Together?

- There are options for how we can work together in your classroom. Let's talk through these options and pick some that feel right to you.
- There are also options for how we can collect student evidence when we are working together in the classroom. How would you like to go about doing this?
- How will we reflect, both individually and collectively, about our work and students' growth?

III. How Will We Approach Co-Planning?

- We will need at least thirty-five to forty minutes each week for planning. What time works for you?
- It is helpful to create a planning system that works for you. How would you like to share this information? (Google Docs, planning template, etc.)

Protocol for Unpacking Standards
Based on Knowledge, Reasoning, and Skills

1. Once a goal for the coaching cycle has been determined, refer to the standard or standards that will be addressed. Pose the question: "What will students need to know and be able to do in order to meet this goal?"

2. In answering the question, create a list of potential learning targets.

3. Go through the list of targets one by one, asking the following questions:

   - Does this target represent factual or procedural knowledge that is to be acquired? (Knowledge)
   - Does this target require the skillful use or application of knowledge? (Reasoning)
   - Does this target address a performance that must be demonstrated in order to be observed or assessed? (Skill)

4. Use the word bank along with these questions to help you categorize and refine the list of targets.

Knowledge	Reasoning	Skill
Explain, understand, describe, identify, name, tell, define, recall, match, know, recognize, label	Analyze, compare/contrast, synthesize, classify, infer/deduce, evaluate, interpret	Listen, perform, conduct, read, speak, assemble, operate, measure, model, use, conduct

Stiggins, Arter, Chappuis, & Chappuis (2006)

Protocol for Sorting Student Work

1. If possible, make a copy of the set of class work for each participant. Otherwise, make fewer copies for participants to examine in pairs. Alternatively, the work can be divided among the group, and participants can write comments on sticky notes before passing their stack to the next person.

2. Read through the entire set of class work, looking for trends relative to the learning targets.

3. Discuss the trends that were noticed. Collectively, decide which ones are the most significant and needing further instruction—either whole or small group.

4. Go back to the work to sort students according to the identified needs. If something pertains to the whole class, this will be addressed in whole group instruction.

5. Plan for instruction based on the needs of each group.

Protocol for Providing Strengths-Based Feedback in Teams

Purpose: Provide strengths-based feedback on a lesson plan, student work, or a unit of study.

1. **Presentation of Your Work (5–10 minutes)**

    The presenting teacher shares any of the following: an upcoming lesson, student data, a unit of study, a set of learning targets, or so on. Participants listen and take notes.

2. **Clarifying Questions (5 minutes)**

    Participants ask clarifying questions. Clarifying may sound like "Did I hear you say . . . ?" or "Can you tell me more about . . . ?"

3. **Value Statements (5 minutes)**

   Participants make statements that highlight positive aspects of the plan. Valuing may sound like "It sounds like you have . . . " "There is a lot of evidence of . . . " or "You have developed . . . "

4. **Possibility Thinking (10 minutes)**

   Participants discuss the "and," or next step, that will take the presenter further in their work. To do so, they build off of what's working already. Possibility thinking may sound like "Where to next?" "How can we help?" "Would it make sense to . . . ?" Comments are made in an invitational manner, therefore sending the signal that the presenting teacher maintains ownership over what happens in the classroom.

RESOURCE F—RESULTS-BASED COACHING TOOL

Results-Based Coaching Tool

Teacher:		Coach:	
Coaching Cycle Focus:		Dates of Coaching Cycle:	
Standards-Based Goal What is the goal for student learning?	**Focus for Teacher Learning** What instructional practices will help students reach the goal?	**Student-Centered Coaching** What coaching practices were implemented during this coaching cycle?	**Student Learning** How did student achievement increase as a result of the coaching cycle?
Students will . . . *Standard(s):* *Learning Targets:* I can: *Baseline Data:* ___ Emerging ___ Developing ___ Meeting ___ Exceeding ___ % of students were able to demonstrate proficiency of the learning targets.	Teacher will . . .	Coach and Teacher did . . . (check those that apply) ☐ Goal setting ☐ Creating learning targets ☐ Analysis of student work ☐ Co-teaching ☐ Collecting student evidence during the class period ☐ Collaborative planning ☐ Shared learning to build knowledge of content and pedagogy	Students are . . . *Post-Assessment Data:* ___ Emerging ___ Developing ___ Meeting ___ Exceeding ___ % of students were able to demonstrate proficiency of the learning targets. *Follow up for students who didn't reach the goal:*

Teacher is . . .

Reflection Questions for the Results-Based Coaching Tool

Teacher Reflections	Coach Reflections
What worked well for you during our collaboration and coaching cycle? How has your teaching been positively impacted?	What worked well for you during our collaboration and coaching cycle?
How do you feel our collaboration has positively impacted the students?	How do you feel our collaboration positively impacted the students?
What were any challenges or missed opportunities during our work together?	What were any challenges or missed opportunities during our work together?
What are some next steps in your teaching?	What are some next steps in my coaching?

References

Barth, R. (2007). *Educational Leadership.* San Francisco, CA: Jossey-Bass.

Beers, K., & Probst, R. (2013). *Notice and note: Strategies for close reading.* Portsmouth, NH: Heinemann.

Beers, K., & Probst, R. (2015). *Reading nonfiction: Notice and note, stances, signposts, and strategies.* Portsmouth, NH: Heinemann.

Brookhart, S., & Moss, C. (2014). Learning targets on parade. *Educational Leadership, 72(2),* 28–33.

Brown, B. (2012). *Daring greatly: How the courage to be vulnerable transforms the way we live, love, parent, and lead.* New York, NY: Gotham Books.

Cheliotes, L., & Reilly, M. (2010). *Coaching conversations: Transforming your school one conversation at a time.* Thousand Oaks, CA: Corwin.

Cook, L., & Friend, M. (1995). Co-teaching: Guidelines for creating effective practices. *Focus on Exceptional Children, 28(3).*

Cuban, L. (2011). *Jazz, basketball, and teacher decision-making.* Retrieved from http://www.larrycuban.wordpress.com/2011/06/16/jazz-basketball-and-teacher-decision-making/

Frey, N., & Fisher, D. (2013). *Rigorous reading: 5 access points for comprehending complex texts.* Thousand Oaks, CA: Corwin.

Glover, M., & Keene, E. (2015). *The teacher you want to be: Essays about children, learning, and teaching.* Portsmouth, NH: Heinemann.

Hattie, J. (2012). *Visible learning for teachers: Maximizing impact on learning.* Thousand Oaks, CA: Corwin.

Imel, S. (2002). *Metacognitive skills for adult learning.* Eric Clearinghouse on Adult, Career, and Vocational Education. Washington DC: Office of Educational Research and Improvement.

Keene, E., & Zimmerman, S. (1997). *Mosaic of thought.* Portsmouth, NH: Heinemann.

Killion, J. (2008). *Assessing impact: Evaluating staff development.* Thousand Oaks, CA: Corwin.

Killion, J., & Harrison, C. (2006). *Taking the lead: New roles for teachers and school-based coaches.* Oxford, OH: National Staff Development Council.

Knight, J. (2007). *Instructional coaching: A partnership approach to improving instruction.* Thousand Oaks, CA: Corwin.

Lai, E. (2011). *Metacognition: A literature review*. Pearson Research Reports. Retrieved from http://images.pearsonassessments.com/images/tmrs/Metacognition_Literature_Review_Final.pdf

Lemov, D. (2010). *Teach like a champion: 49 techniques that put students on the path to college.* San Francisco, CA: Jossey-Bass.

Parcells, B. (2001). The tough work of turning around a team. *Harvard Business Review on Turnarounds* (pp. 105–114). Boston, MA: Harvard School Press.

Park, L. S. (2010). *A long walk to water.* Boston, MA: Clarion Books.

Pearson, P. D., & Gallagher, M. C. (1983). The instruction of reading comprehension. *Contemporary Educational Psychology, 8,* 317–344.

Pollock, J. (2012). *Feedback: The hinge that joins teaching and learning.* Thousand Oaks, CA: Corwin.

Reeves, A. (2011). *Where great teaching begins: Planning for student thinking and learning.* Alexandria, VA: ASCD.

Sadder, M., & Nidus, G. (2009). *The literacy coach's game plan.* Newark, DE: International Reading Association.

Schlechty, P. (2011). *Engaging students: The next level of working on the work.* San Francisco, CA: John Wiley & Sons.

Stiggins, R., Arter, J., Chappuis, J., Chappuis, S. (2006). *Classroom assessment for student learning: Doing it right—Using it well.* Portland, OR: Assessment Training Institute.

Stone, D., & Heen, S. (2015). *Thanks for the feedback: The science and art of receiving feedback well.* New York, NY: Penguin Books.

Sweeney, D. (2011). *Student-centered coaching: A guide for K–8 coaches and principals.* Thousand Oaks, CA: Corwin.

Sweeney, D. (2013). *Student-centered coaching at the secondary level.* Thousand Oaks, CA: Corwin.

Tomlinson, C. A. (2014). The bridge between today's lesson and tomorrow's. *Educational Leadership, 71*(6), 10–14.

Vygotsky, L. S. (1978). *Mind in society: The development of higher psychological processes.* Cambridge, MA: Harvard University Press.

Webb, N. (1997). *Research monograph number 6: Criteria for alignment of expectations and assessments on mathematics and science education.* Washington, DC: CCSSO.

West, L. (2008). *Content Coaching: Mentoring, coaching, and collaboration.* Thousand Oaks, CA: Corwin.

Wiggins, G., & McTighe, J. (2005). *Understanding by design* (2nd ed.). Alexandria, VA: ASCD.

Wiliam, D. (2011). *Embedded formative assessment.* Bloomington, IN: Solution Tree Press.

Index

Academic rigor, 28
Advice-giving behaviors, 93, 93 (figure), 94 (figure)
Anecdotal evidence, 71, 72 (figure)
Appreciative feedback, 120, 121 (figure)
Arter, J., 40, 60, 163
Assessment alignment strategies, 30–31, 136–138, 137 (figure)

Backward design, 25
Barth, R., 56
Beers, K., 98
Brookhart, S., 26–27
Brown, B., 117, 118

Celebrate success, 141
Chappuis, J., 40, 60, 163
Chappuis, S., 40, 60, 163
Cheliotes, L., 117
Clarification strategies, 120, 121 (figure), 129 (figure), 130 (figure), 163
Classroom coaching
  collaborative planning and preparation, 45–47, 46 (figure), 49, 50 (figure)
  co-teaching approach, 43–50
  effective language, 55, 55 (figure)
  instructional pace, 49–50
  partnership agreements, 44–45, 56, 56 (figure), 162
  practical examples, 52–55, 54 (figure)
  student-centered learning targets, 48–49
Coaching beliefs, 1–3
Coaching cycles
  basic concepts, 9–10
  components, 9
  contextual influences, 75–76
  co-teaching approach, 43–50
  effective goal-setting conversations, 12–20, 13–14 (figure), 15 (figure)
  functional role, 3
  instructional pace, 49–50
  measuring the impact step, 134–144, 137 (figure), 139 (figure), 145–147 (figure), 148
  micro modeling, 76–88
  partnership agreements, 162
  shared thinking, 92–96, 93 (figure), 94 (figure)
  small groups, 19–20, 78, 96, 97 (figure)
  sorting student work, 103–110
  stages, 135 (figure)
  strengths-based feedback, 119–123
  see also Goal-setting strategies; Standards-based learning targets
Coaching logs, 22, 22 (figure), 156–157
Co-conferring option, 46 (figure), 63, 78, 98–99
Collaborative behaviors, 93, 94–95
  see also Thinking aloud
Collaborative learning, 129, 129–130 (figure)
Conference notes, 70, 71 (figure), 157
Conferring practices, 63, 78, 96, 97 (figure), 98–99
Cook, L., 43–44
Co-planning approach
  intentionality, 49, 49 (figure)
  language stems, 158
  learning targets, 161
  micro modeling, 79–80, 81 (figure)
  noticing and naming, 66–67
  partnership agreements, 56, 56 (figure), 162
  planning tools, 161
  sorting student work, 105
  student-centered learning targets, 36, 39, 39–40 (figure)

Costner, Kevin, 133
Co-teaching approach
  background, 43–44
  benefits, 4
  collaborative planning and preparation, 45–47, 46 (figure), 49, 50 (figure)
  effective language, 55, 55 (figure)
  instructional pace, 49–50
  micro modeling, 77
  partnership agreements, 44–45, 56, 56 (figure), 162
  practical examples, 52–55, 54 (figure)
  student-centered learning targets, 48–49
Cuban, L., 91

Data collection and analysis, 105–109
Deep learning and understanding, 17
Depth of Knowledge (DOK) framework, 28, 29 (figure)
Dewey, John, 136
Differentiating instruction, 14

Effective goal-setting conversations, 12–20, 13–14 (figure), 15 (figure)
Engaged students, 16, 47, 63
Exit interviews, 139, 139 (figure), 160
Exit tickets, 107 (figure), 107–108

Feedback, 60, 117, 118–119
  see also Noticing and naming; Reflective feedback; Results-Based Coaching Tool; Strengths-based feedback
Field of Dreams (film), 133
Fisher, D., 63
Focused lessons, 80, 82
Formative assessments
  functional role, 104–105
  importance, 60
  measuring the impact of coaching, 137–138
  measuring the impact, 137–138
  noticing and naming, 63–65, 64 (figure), 105
  sorting student work, 104–110
  student-centered coaching, 4–5, 104–105
  see also Thinking aloud
Four square planner, 115, 115 (figure), 161
Frey, N., 63
Friend, M., 43–44

Gallagher, M. C., 77
Getting ready for coaching step
  background, 43–44
  effective language, 55, 55 (figure)
  if/then charts, 55 (figure)
  importance, 44–45
  key characteristics, 45–52
  partnership agreements, 56, 56 (figure)
  practical examples, 52–55, 54 (figure)
Glover, M., 149
Goal-setting strategies
  benefits, 3
  coaching logs, 22, 22 (figure), 156–157
  effective goal-setting conversations, 12–20, 13–14 (figure), 15 (figure)
  if/then charts, 22, 22 (figure)
  importance, 10–11
  language stems, 158
  learning outcomes, 11, 12 (figure)
  micro modeling, 80, 82
  open-ended questions, 23
  practical examples, 20–21
  shared thinking, 95–96
  stages, 11 (figure)
  standards-based goals, 10–11, 16, 19
Goldilocks goals, 16–17, 17 (figure)
Gradual Release of Responsibility model, 77
Graphic organizers, 98, 116
Group instruction, 78, 96, 97 (figure)

Harrison, C., 44
Hattie, J., 60
Heen, S., 119
Hidden agendas, 121
High-stakes assessments, 5

If/then charts
  getting ready for coaching step, 55 (figure)
  goal-setting strategies, 22 (figure)
  learning targets, 38 (figure)
  measuring the impact step, 144, 147 (figure), 155 (figure)
  micro modeling, 85 (figure), 153 (figure)
  noticing and naming, 70 (figure), 152 (figure)
  sorting student work, 114 (figure), 154 (figure)
  strengths-based feedback, 128 (figure), 154 (figure)
  thinking aloud, 100 (figure), 153 (figure)
Imel, S., 90
Implementation practices, 78–79
Individual instruction, 78, 96, 97 (figure)
Instructional expectations, 19
Instructional pace, 49–50
Intellectual rigor, 28

Jones, James Earl, 133
Judgmental thinking, 121
"Just right" goals
  see Goldilocks goals

Keene, E., 89, 149
Killion, J., 44, 135
Knight, J., 12
Knowledge skills, 39 (figure),
  41 (figure), 162–163

Lai, E., 92
Language stems, 100, 130 (figure), 158–160
Learning targets
  agreements and protocols, 162–163
  assessment alignment strategies, 30–31,
    136–138, 137 (figure)
  benefits, 3, 26–27, 48–49
  coaching logs, 156–157
  co-planning strategies, 36, 39,
    39–40 (figure), 161
  developmental process, 27–28,
    29 (figure)
  effective language, 38, 38 (figure)
  evidentiary information, 50–52,
    51–52 (figure)
  guiding questions, 39, 39 (figure)
  if/then charts, 38 (figure)
  micro modeling, 81 (figure)
  noticing and naming, 61–63, 62 (figure),
    67–68, 68–69 (figure)
  planning tools, 161
  practical examples, 33–38, 35 (figure)
  self-evaluation rubrics, 32–33 (figure),
    32–33
  strengths-based feedback, 120,
    121 (figure)
  student evidence, 106–108, 107 (figure)
  unpacking standards, 29–30, 31 (figure),
    40, 41 (figure)
Lemov, D., 107
Lessons From the Field
  co-teaching approach, 52–55, 54 (figure)
  effective goal-setting conversations,
    20–21
  measuring the impact,
    142–144
  micro modeling, 82–85, 84 (figure)
  noticing and naming, 67–70,
    68 (figure)
  sorting student work, 110–114,
    112 (figure)
  standards-based learning targets, 33–38,
    35 (figure)

strengths-based feedback, 123–125,
  125 (figure), 126–127 (figure), 127–128
thinking aloud, 97–99
Long Walk to Water, A (Park), 111

McTighe, J., 25
Measuring the impact
  assessment alignment strategies,
    136–138, 137 (figure)
  benefits, 148
  challenges, 144
  effective language, 148 (figure)
  functional role, 134
  if/then charts, 148 (figure), 155 (figure)
  importance, 134–136
  key characteristics, 136–141
  ongoing support, 139–140
  practical examples, 142–144
  self-reflection, 140–141
  teacher reflection and growth, 138–141,
    139 (figure), 147 (figure),
    165–166 (figure)
Metacognitive thinking, 89–95
Micro modeling
  co-teaching approach, 46 (figure)
  effective language, 85, 85 (figure)
  functional role, 76–77
  if/then charts, 85 (figure), 153 (figure)
  importance, 77
  key characteristics, 78–80,
    81 (figure), 82
  language stems, 158–159
  practical examples, 82–85, 84 (figure)
  reflective questions, 87 (figure), 88
  video use, 86 (figure), 87
Mixed messages, 121
Modeling impacts, 47–48, 88, 94–95
Moss, C., 26–27

Nidus, G., 79
Note-taking strategy, 50–52, 51–52 (figure)
Noticing and naming
  anecdotal evidence, 72, 72–73 (figure)
  basic concepts, 59–60
  coaching logs, 156–157
  conference notes, 71, 71–72 (figure)
  co-planning strategies, 67
  co-teaching approach, 46 (figure), 51
  effective language, 70, 70–71 (figure)
  formative assessments, 63–65,
    64 (figure), 105
  functional role, 67
  if/then charts, 70–71 (figure), 152 (figure)
  importance, 60–61

learning targets, 61–63, 62 (figure), 67–70, 68 (figure)
planning guidelines, 65–66, 66 (figure)
practical examples, 67–70, 68 (figure)
tools and techniques, 70–71 (figure), 70–72, 71–72 (figure)

Observational impacts, 47–48, 121–122
One-on-one instruction, 78, 96, 97 (figure)
Ongoing support, 139–140
Open-ended questions, 23, 93 (figure)

Parcells, B., 9
Park, L. S., 111
Partnerships
   agreements and protocols, 162–164
   co-teaching, 4, 43–45, 56, 56 (figure), 77
   effective goal-setting conversations, 12–20, 13–14 (figure), 15 (figure)
   supportive environments, 4
Pearson, P. D., 77
Performance skills, 39 (figure), 41 (figure), 162–163
Personal reflection, 129, 129 (figure), 134
Planning tools, 81 (figure), 161
Pollock, J., 60
Post-assessments, 36, 36–37 (figure), 38, 136–137, 137 (figure)
Pre-assessments, 35, 35 (figure), 104–105, 136–137, 137 (figure)
Probst, R., 98
Professional learning communities (PLCs), 20, 109
Progress monitoring, 5
Project-oriented goals, 18
Public Education & Business Coalition (PEBC), 89

Reasoning skills, 39 (figure), 41 (figure), 162–163
Reeves, A., 28
Reflective feedback
   experiential reflection, 136
   framework, 117–118
   personal reflection, 129, 129 (figure), 134
   teacher reflection and growth, 138–141, 139 (figure), 147 (figure)
Reframing skills, 13–14
Reilly, M., 117
Relationship-driven coaching, 5–6, 7, 11, 12 (figure)

Response to Intervention (RTI) system, 138
Results-Based Coaching Tool, 142, 143, 144, 145–147 (figure), 165–166 (figure)
Rubrics, 32–33 (figure), 32–33

Sadder, M., 79
Scaffolding, 14
Schlechty, P., 16
School leaders, 4
Self-evaluation rubrics, 32–33 (figure), 32–33
Self-reflection, 140–141
Shared decision-making, 78, 79–80, 81 (figure)
Shared thinking
   see Thinking aloud
Sharing lessons, 81 (figure), 161
Sharing success, 141
Signposts, 97–99
Small-group coaching cycles, 19–20, 78, 96, 97 (figure)
SMART goals, 18
Sorting student work
   agreements and protocols, 163
   criteria checklist, 116, 116 (figure)
   effective language, 114, 114 (figure)
   four square planner, 115 (figure), 116, 161
   functional role, 104, 108–109
   if/then charts, 154 (figure)
   importance, 104–105
   key characteristics, 105–110
   practical examples, 109 (figure), 110–114, 112 (figure)
   team approach, 109–110
   see also Data collection and analysis
Standards-based goals, 10–11, 16, 19
Standards-based learning targets
   agreements and protocols, 162–163
   assessment alignment strategies, 30–31, 136–138, 137 (figure), 156–157
   benefits, 3, 26–27, 48–49
   co-planning strategies, 36, 39, 39–40 (figure), 161
   developmental process, 27–28, 29 (figure)
   effective language, 38, 38 (figure)
   guiding questions, 39, 39 (figure)
   if/then charts, 38 (figure)
   micro modeling, 81 (figure)
   noticing and naming, 61–63, 62 (figure), 67–70, 68 (figure)

planning tools, 161
practical examples, 33–38, 35 (figure)
self-evaluation rubrics, 32–33 (figure), 32–33
strengths-based feedback, 120, 121 (figure)
student evidence, 106–108, 107 (figure)
unpacking standards, 29–30, 31 (figure), 40, 41 (figure)
using student evidence, 50–52, 51–52 (figure)
Stiggins, R., 40, 60, 163
Stone, D., 119
Strengths-based feedback
 agreements and protocols, 163–164
 challenges, 121–122
 clarification strategies, 120, 121 (figure), 129 (figure), 130 (figure), 163
 collaborative learning, 129, 129–130 (figure)
 effective language, 121 (figure), 128, 128 (figure), 130 (figure), 130–131
 functional role, 118
 if/then charts, 128 (figure), 154 (figure)
 importance, 60, 117, 118–119
 key characteristics, 119–123
 language stems, 130 (figure), 159–160
 learning targets, 120, 121 (figure)
 personal reflection, 129, 129 (figure)
 practical examples, 123–125, 125 (figure), 126–127 (figure), 127–128
 uncovering possibilities, 120, 121 (figure), 130 (figure), 164
 value statements, 120, 121 (figure), 130 (figure), 164
Strengths-based relationships, 82
Student-centered coaching
 core practices, 3–4
 formative assessments, 4–5, 104–105
 implementation practices, 78–79
 learning outcomes, 11, 12 (figure)
 measurement approaches, 4
 model comparisons, 5–7
 shared thinking, 92–96, 93 (figure), 94 (figure)
 stages, 135 (figure)
 strengths-based feedback, 119–123
 see also Micro modeling
Student-centered learning targets
 agreements and protocols, 162–163
 assessment alignment strategies, 30–31, 136–138, 137 (figure), 156–157
 benefits, 3, 26–27, 48–49

co-planning strategies, 36, 39, 39–40 (figure), 161
developmental process, 27–28, 29 (figure)
effective language, 38, 38 (figure)
guiding questions, 39, 39 (figure)
if/then charts, 38 (figure)
micro modeling, 81 (figure)
noticing and naming, 61–63, 62 (figure), 67–68, 68–69 (figure)
planning tools, 161
practical examples, 33–38, 35 (figure)
self-evaluation rubrics, 32–33 (figure), 32–33
strengths-based feedback, 120, 121 (figure)
student evidence, 106–108, 107 (figure)
unpacking standards, 29–30, 31 (figure), 40, 41 (figure)
using student evidence, 50–52, 51–52 (figure)
Student engagement, 16, 47, 63
Student evidence
 collaborative planning and preparation, 47
 criteria checklist, 116, 116 (figure)
 efficient practices, 108
 functional role, 4
 learning targets, 106–108, 107 (figure)
 note-taking strategy, 50–52, 51–52 (figure)
 noticing and naming, 61–63, 62 (figure), 65–66, 66 (figure), 71–72, 71–72 (figure), 72–73 (figure)
 sorting student work, 103–110, 109 (figure), 112 (figure), 114 (figure), 115 (figure), 116, 116 (figure)
 see also Measuring the impact step
Summative assessments, 5
Supportive environments, 4, 139–140
Sweeney, D., 6, 9, 16, 50, 77, 105, 118, 134

Tandem teaching option, 46 (figure), 51
Task-oriented goals, 18
Teacher-centered coaching, 5–7, 11, 12 (figure)
Teacher reflection and growth, 138–141, 139 (figure), 147 (figure), 165–166 (figure)
Teaching and learning cycle, 105
Telemark skiing example, 118–119
Thinking aloud
 background, 89
 co-teaching approach, 46 (figure)

effective language, 99, 100 (figure)
if/then charts, 100 (figure), 153 (figure)
importance, 91
key characteristics, 91–97, 93 (figure), 94 (figure), 97 (figure)
language stems, 100, 159
metacognitive thinking, 89–95
practical examples, 97–99
stem examples, 100
Tomlinson, C. A., 4
Tools and Techniques
co-teaching approach, 55 (figure), 55–56
effective goal-setting conversations, 22 (figure), 22–23
learning targets, 38 (figure), 38–40
measuring the impact step, 144, 145–147 (figure)
micro modeling, 85, 85 (figure), 86 (figure), 87, 88
noticing and naming, 70–71 (figure), 70–72, 71–72 (figure)
sorting student work, 114, 114 (figure)
strengths-based feedback, 128–131
thinking aloud, 99–100, 100 (figure)
Trust, 82

Uncovering possibilities
 see Strengths-Based Feedback
Understanding By Design (UbD), 25
Unpacking standards, 29–30, 31 (figure), 40, 41 (figure), 158, 162–163

Value statements, 120, 121 (figure), 130 (figure), 164
Video clips, 86 (figure), 87
Visible learning, 106–108, 107 (figure)
Vygotsky, L. S., 122

Webb, N., 28
Webb's theory of the Depth of Knowledge, 28, 29 (figure)
West, L., 78
Whole group instruction, 78, 96, 97 (figure)
Wiggins, G., 25
Wiliam, D., 104
Word banks, 41 (figure), 163

You Pick Four option, 46 (figure), 47

Zimmerman, S., 89
Zone of Proximal Development (ZPD), 122–123, 123 (figure)

Helping educators make the greatest impact

CORWIN HAS ONE MISSION: to enhance education through intentional professional learning.

We build long-term relationships with our authors, educators, clients, and associations who partner with us to develop and continuously improve the best evidence-based practices that establish and support lifelong learning.

Solutions you want. Experts you trust. Results you need.

AUTHOR CONSULTING

Author Consulting

On-site professional learning with sustainable results! Let us help you design a professional learning plan to meet the unique needs of your school or district. www.corwin.com/pd

INSTITUTES

Institutes

Corwin Institutes provide collaborative learning experiences that equip your team with tools and action plans ready for immediate implementation. www.corwin.com/institutes

eCOURSES

eCourses

Practical, flexible online professional learning designed to let you go at your own pace. www.corwin.com/ecourses

READ2EARN

Read2Earn

Did you know you can earn graduate credit for reading this book? Find out how: www.corwin.com/read2earn

---

Contact an account manager at (800) 831-6640 or visit **www.corwin.com** for more information.